THIS BOOK
BELONGS TO

....

....

Author's Afterthoughts

With so many books out there to choose from, I want to thank you for choosing this one and taking precious time out of your life to buy and read my work. Readers like you are the reason I take such passion in creating these books.

It is with gratitude and humility that I express how honored I am to become a part of your life and I hope that you take the same pleasure in reading this book as I did in writing it.

Can I ask one small favour? I ask that you write an honest and open review on Amazon of what you thought of the book. This will help other readers make an informed choice on whether to buy this book.

My sincerest thanks.

@COPYRIGHT 2024

The content contained within this book may not be reproduced, duplicated, or transmitted without direct written permission from the author or the publisher. Under no circumstances will any blame or legal responsibility be held against the publisher, or author, for any damages, reparation, or monetary loss due to the information contained within this book. Either directly or indirectly.

Legal Notice:

This book is copyright protected. This book is only for personal use. You cannot amend, distribute, sell, use, quote, or paraphrase any part, or the content within this book, without the consent of the author or publisher.

Disclaimer Notice:

Please note the information contained within this document is for educational and entertainment purposes only. All effort has been executed to present accurate, up-to-date, and reliable, complete information. No warranties of any kind are declared or implied. Readers acknowledge that the author is not engaging in the rendering of legal, financial, medical, or professional advice. The content within this book has been derived from various sources. Please consult a licensed professional before attempting any techniques outlined in this book. By reading this document, the reader agrees that under no circumstances is the author responsible for any losses, direct or indirect, which are incurred as a result of the use of the information contained within this document, including, but not limited to — errors, omissions, or inaccuracies.

Table of Contents

Goals of the Style Guide	5
C++ Version	8
Header Files	8
Scoping	15
Classes	29
Functions	43
Other C++ Features	52
Naming	95
Comments	103
Formatting	113
Exceptions to the Rules	137
Parting Words	139

Background

C++ is one of the main development languages used by many of open-source projects. As every C++ programmer knows, the language has many powerful features, but this power brings with it complexity, which in turn can make code more bug-prone and harder to read and maintain.

The goal of this guide is to manage this complexity by describing in detail the dos and don'ts of writing C++ code . These rules exist to keep the code base manageable while still allowing coders to use C++ language features productively.

Style, also known as readability, is what we call the conventions that govern our C++ code. The term Style is a bit of a misnomer since these conventions cover far more than just source file formatting.

Most open-source projects developed conform to the requirements in this guide.

Note that this guide is not a C++ tutorial: we assume that the reader is familiar with the language.

Goals of the Style Guide

Why do we have this document?

There are a few core goals that we believe this guide should serve. These are the fundamental **why**s that underlie all of the individual rules. By bringing these ideas to the fore, we hope to ground discussions and make it clearer to our broader community why the rules are in place and why particular decisions have been made. If you understand what goals each rule is serving, it should be clearer to everyone when a rule may be waived (some can be), and what sort of argument or alternative would be necessary to change a rule in the guide.

The goals of the style guide as we currently see them are as follows:
Style rules should pull their weight

The benefit of a style rule must be large enough to justify asking all of our engineers to remember it. The benefit is measured relative to the codebase we would get without the rule, so a rule against a very harmful practice may still have a small benefit if people are unlikely to do it anyway. This principle mostly explains the rules we don't have, rather than the rules we do: for example, goto contravenes many of the following principles, but is already vanishingly rare, so the Style Guide doesn't discuss it.

Optimize for the reader, not the writer

Our codebase (and most individual components submitted to it) is expected to continue for quite some time. As a result, more time will be spent reading most of our code than writing it. We explicitly choose to optimize for the experience of our average software engineer reading, maintaining, and debugging code in our codebase rather than ease when writing said code. "Leave a trace for the reader" is a particularly common sub-point of this principle: When something surprising or unusual is happening in a snippet of code (for example, transfer of pointer ownership), leaving textual hints for the reader at the point of use is valuable (std::unique_ptr demonstrates the ownership transfer unambiguously at the call site).

Be consistent with existing code

Using one style consistently through our codebase lets us focus on other (more important) issues. Consistency also allows for automation: tools that format your code or adjust your #include s only work properly when your code is consistent with the expectations of the tooling. In many cases, rules that are attributed to "Be Consistent" boil down to "Just pick one and stop worrying about it"; the potential value of allowing flexibility on these points is outweighed by the cost of having people argue over them.

Be consistent with the broader C++ community when appropriate

Consistency with the way other organizations use C++ has value for the same reasons as consistency within our code base. If a feature in the C++ standard solves a problem, or if some idiom is widely known and accepted, that's an argument for using it. However, sometimes standard features and idioms are flawed, or were just designed without our codebase's needs in mind. In those cases (as described below) it's appropriate to constrain or ban standard features. In some cases we prefer a homegrown or third-party library over a library defined in the C++ Standard, either out of perceived superiority or insufficient value to transition the codebase to the standard interface.

Avoid surprising or dangerous constructs

C++ has features that are more surprising or dangerous than one might think at a glance. Some style guide restrictions are in place to prevent falling into these pitfalls. There is a high bar for style guide waivers on such restrictions, because waiving such rules often directly risks compromising program correctness.

Avoid constructs that our average C++ programmer would find tricky or hard to maintain

C++ has features that may not be generally appropriate because of the complexity they introduce to the code. In widely used code, it may be more acceptable to use trickier language constructs, because any benefits of more complex implementation are multiplied widely by usage, and the cost in understanding the complexity does not need to be paid again when working with new portions of the codebase. When in doubt, waivers to rules of this type can be sought by asking your project leads. This is specifically important for our codebase because code ownership and team membership changes over time: even if everyone that works with some piece of code currently understands it, such understanding is not guaranteed to hold a few years from now.

Be mindful of our scale
: With a codebase of 100+ million lines and thousands of engineers, some mistakes and simplifications for one engineer can become costly for many. For instance it's particularly important to avoid polluting the global namespace: name collisions across a codebase of hundreds of millions of lines are difficult to work with and hard to avoid if everyone puts things into the global namespace.

Concede to optimization when necessary
: Performance optimizations can sometimes be necessary and appropriate, even when they conflict with the other principles of this document.

The intent of this document is to provide maximal guidance with reasonable restriction. As always, common sense and good taste should prevail. By this we specifically refer to the established conventions of the entire C++ community, not just your personal preferences or those of your team. Be skeptical about and reluctant to use clever or unusual constructs: the absence of a prohibition is not the same as a license to proceed. Use your judgment, and if you are unsure, please don't hesitate to ask your project leads to get additional input.

C++ Version

Currently, code should target C++17, i.e., should not use C++2x features. The C++ version targeted by this guide will advance (aggressively) over time.

Do not use non-standard extensions.

Consider portability to other environments before using features from C++14 and C++17 in your project.

Header Files

In general, every .cc file should have an associated .h file. There are some common exceptions, such as unittests and small .cc files containing just a main() function.

Correct use of header files can make a huge difference to the readability, size and performance of your code.

The following rules will guide you through the various pitfalls of using header files.

Self-contained Headers

Header files should be self-contained (compile on their own) and end in .h . Non-header files that are meant for inclusion should end in .inc and be used sparingly.

All header files should be self-contained. Users and refactoring tools should not have to adhere to special conditions to include the header. Specifically, a header should have header guards and include all other headers it needs.

Prefer placing the definitions for template and inline functions in the same file as their declarations. The definitions of these constructs must be included into every .cc file that uses them, or the program may fail to link in some build configurations. If declarations and definitions are in different files, including the former should transitively include the latter. Do not move these definitions to separately included header files (-inl.h); this practice was common in the past, but is no longer allowed.

As an exception, a template that is explicitly instantiated for all relevant sets of template arguments, or that is a private implementation detail of a class, is allowed to be defined in the one and only .cc file that instantiates the template.

There are rare cases where a file designed to be included is not self-contained. These are typically intended to be included at unusual locations, such as the middle of another file. They might not use header guards, and might not include their prerequisites. Name such files with the .inc extension. Use sparingly, and prefer self-contained headers when possible.

The #define Guard

All header files should have #define guards to prevent multiple inclusion. The format of the symbol name should be *<PROJECT>_<PATH>_<FILE>_H_* .

To guarantee uniqueness, they should be based on the full path in a project's source tree. For example, the file foo/src/bar/baz.h in project foo should have the following guard:

```
#ifndef FOO_BAR_BAZ_H_
#define FOO_BAR_BAZ_H_

...

#endif // FOO_BAR_BAZ_H_
```

Forward Declarations

Avoid using forward declarations where possible.
Instead, #include the headers you need.

A "forward declaration" is a declaration of a class, function, or template without an associated definition.

- Forward declarations can save compile time, as #include s force the compiler to open more files and process more input.
- Forward declarations can save on unnecessary recompilation. #include s can force your code to be recompiled more often, due to unrelated changes in the header.

- Forward declarations can hide a dependency, allowing user code to skip necessary recompilation when headers change.
- A forward declaration may be broken by subsequent changes to the library. Forward declarations of functions and templates can prevent the header owners from making otherwise-compatible changes to their APIs, such as widening a parameter type, adding a template parameter with a default value, or migrating to a new namespace.
- Forward declaring symbols from namespace std:: yields undefined behavior.
- It can be difficult to determine whether a forward declaration or a full #include is needed. Replacing an #include with a forward declaration can silently change the meaning of code:

```
// b.h:
struct B {};
struct D : B {};

// good_user.cc:
#include "b.h"
void f(B*);
void f(void*);
void test(D* x) { f(x); }  // calls f(B*)
```

If the #include was replaced with forward decls for B and D, test() would call f(void*).

- Forward declaring multiple symbols from a header can be more verbose than simply #include ing the header.
- Structuring code to enable forward declarations (e.g. using pointer members instead of object members) can make the code slower and more complex.

- Try to avoid forward declarations of entities defined in another project.
- When using a function declared in a header file, always #include that header.
- When using a class template, prefer to #include its header file.

Please see <u>Names and Order of Includes</u> for rules about when to #include a header.

Inline Functions

Define functions inline only when they are small, say, 10 lines or fewer.

You can declare functions in a way that allows the compiler to expand them inline rather than calling them through the usual function call mechanism.

Inlining a function can generate more efficient object code, as long as the inlined function is small. Feel free to inline accessors and mutators, and other short, performance-critical functions.

Overuse of inlining can actually make programs slower. Depending on a function's size, inlining it can cause the code size to increase or decrease. Inlining a very small accessor function will usually decrease code size while inlining a very large function can dramatically increase code size. On modern processors smaller code usually runs faster due to better use of the instruction cache.

A decent rule of thumb is to not inline a function if it is more than 10 lines long. Beware of destructors, which are often longer than they appear because of implicit member- and base-destructor calls!

Another useful rule of thumb: it's typically not cost effective to inline functions with loops or switch statements (unless, in the common case, the loop or switch statement is never executed).

It is important to know that functions are not always inlined even if they are declared as such; for example, virtual and recursive functions are not normally inlined. Usually recursive functions should not be inline. The main reason for making a virtual function inline is to place its definition in the class, either for convenience or to document its behavior, e.g., for accessors and mutators.

Names and Order of Includes

Include headers in the following order: Related header, C system headers, C++ standard library headers, other libraries' headers, your project's headers.

All of a project's header files should be listed as descendants of the project's source directory without use of UNIX directory aliases . (the current directory) or .. (the parent directory). For example, awesome-project/src/base/logging.h should be included as:

```
#include "base/logging.h"
```

In *dir/foo*.cc or *dir/foo_test*.cc , whose main purpose is to implement or test the stuff in *dir2/foo2*.h , order your includes as follows:

1. *dir2/foo2*.h .
2. A blank line
3. C system headers (more precisely: headers in angle brackets with the .h extension),
   e.g. <unistd.h> , <stdlib.h> .

4. A blank line
5. C++ standard library headers (without file extension), e.g. `<algorithm>`, `<cstddef>`.
6. A blank line
7. Other libraries' `.h` files.
8. Your project's `.h` files.

Separate each non-empty group with one blank line.

With the preferred ordering, if the related header *dir2/foo2*.h omits any necessary includes, the build of *dir/foo*.cc or *dir/foo_test*.cc will break. Thus, this rule ensures that build breaks show up first for the people working on these files, not for innocent people in other packages.

dir/foo.cc and *dir2/foo2*.h are usually in the same directory (e.g. `base/basictypes_test.cc` and `base/basictypes.h`), but may sometimes be in different directories too.

Note that the C headers such as `stddef.h` are essentially interchangeable with their C++ counterparts (`cstddef`). Either style is acceptable, but prefer consistency with existing code.

Within each section the includes should be ordered alphabetically. Note that older code might not conform to this rule and should be fixed when convenient.

You should include all the headers that define the symbols you rely upon, except in the unusual case of <u>forward declaration</u>. If you rely on symbols from `bar.h`, don't count on the fact that you included `foo.h` which (currently) includes `bar.h`: include `bar.h` yourself, unless `foo.h` explicitly demonstrates its intent to provide you the symbols of `bar.h`.

For example, the includes in `awesome-project/src/foo/internal/fooserver.cc` might look like this:

```
#include "foo/server/fooserver.h"
```

```
#include <sys/types.h>
#include <unistd.h>

#include <string>
#include <vector>

#include "base/basictypes.h"
#include "base/commandlineflags.h"
#include "foo/server/bar.h"
```

Exception:

Sometimes, system-specific code needs conditional includes. Such code can put conditional includes after other includes. Of course, keep your system-specific code small and localized. Example:

```
#include "foo/public/fooserver.h"

#include "base/port.h"  // For LANG_CXX11.

#ifdef LANG_CXX11
#include <initializer_list>
#endif  // LANG_CXX11
```

Scoping

Namespaces

With few exceptions, place code in a namespace. Namespaces should have unique names based on the project name, and possibly its path. Do not use *using-directives* (e.g. using namespace foo). Do not use inline namespaces. For unnamed namespaces, see Unnamed Namespaces and Static Variables.

Namespaces subdivide the global scope into distinct, named scopes, and so are useful for preventing name collisions in the global scope.

Namespaces provide a method for preventing name conflicts in large programs while allowing most code to use reasonably short names.

For example, if two different projects have a class Foo in the global scope, these symbols may collide at compile time or at runtime. If each project places their code in a namespace, project1::Foo and project2::Foo are now distinct symbols that do not collide, and code within each project's namespace can continue to refer to Foo without the prefix.

Inline namespaces automatically place their names in the enclosing scope. Consider the following snippet, for example:

```
namespace outer {
inline namespace inner {
  void foo();
} // namespace inner
} // namespace outer
```

The expressions outer::inner::foo() and outer::foo() are interchangeable. Inline namespaces are primarily intended for ABI compatibility across versions.

Namespaces can be confusing, because they complicate the mechanics of figuring out what definition a name refers to.

Inline namespaces, in particular, can be confusing because names aren't actually restricted to the namespace where they are declared. They are only useful as part of some larger versioning policy.

In some contexts, it's necessary to repeatedly refer to symbols by their fully-qualified names. For deeply-nested namespaces, this can add a lot of clutter.

Namespaces should be used as follows:

- Follow the rules on <u>Namespace Names</u>.
- Terminate namespaces with comments as shown in the given examples.
- Namespaces wrap the entire source file after includes, gflags definitions/declarations and forward declarations of classes from other namespaces.

- // In the .h file
- namespace mynamespace {
-
- // All declarations are within the namespace scope.
- // Notice the lack of indentation.
- class MyClass {
- public:
-   ...
-   void Foo();
- };
-
- } // namespace mynamespace
- // In the .cc file
- namespace mynamespace {
-
- // Definition of functions is within scope of the namespace.
- void MyClass::Foo() {
-   ...
- }
-
- } // namespace mynamespace

More complex .cc files might have additional details, like flags or using-declarations.

```
#include "a.h"

ABSL_FLAG(bool, someflag, false, "dummy flag");

namespace mynamespace {

using ::foo::Bar;

...code for mynamespace...    // Code goes against the left margin.

}  // namespace mynamespace
```

- To place generated protocol message code in a namespace, use the package specifier in the .proto file. See [Protocol Buffer Packages](#) for details.
- Do not declare anything in namespace std, including forward declarations of standard library classes. Declaring entities in namespace std is undefined behavior, i.e., not portable. To declare entities from the standard library, include the appropriate header file.
- You may not use a *using-directive* to make all names from a namespace available.

```
// Forbidden -- This pollutes the namespace.
using namespace foo;
```

- Do not use *Namespace aliases* at namespace scope in header files except in explicitly marked internal-only namespaces, because anything imported into a namespace in a header file becomes part of the public API exported by that file.

- // Shorten access to some commonly used names in .cc files.
- namespace baz = ::foo::bar::baz;
- // Shorten access to some commonly used names (in a .h file).
- namespace librarian {
- namespace impl { // Internal, not part of the API.
- namespace sidetable = ::pipeline_diagnostics::sidetable;
- } // namespace impl
-
- inline void my_inline_function() {
-   // namespace alias local to a function (or method).
-   namespace baz = ::foo::bar::baz;
-   ...
- }
- } // namespace librarian
- Do not use inline namespaces.

Unnamed Namespaces and Static Variables

When definitions in a .cc file do not need to be referenced outside that file, place them in an unnamed namespace or declare them static. Do not use either of these constructs in .h files.

All declarations can be given internal linkage by placing them in unnamed namespaces. Functions and variables can also be given internal linkage by declaring them static. This means that anything you're declaring can't be accessed from another file. If a different file declares something with the same name, then the two entities are completely independent.

Use of internal linkage in .cc files is encouraged for all code that does not need to be referenced elsewhere. Do not use internal linkage in .h files.

Format unnamed namespaces like named namespaces. In the terminating comment, leave the namespace name empty:

```
namespace {
...
}  // namespace
```

Nonmember, Static Member, and Global Functions

Prefer placing nonmember functions in a namespace; use completely global functions rarely. Do not use a class simply to group static functions. Static methods of a class should generally be closely related to instances of the class or the class's static data.

Nonmember and static member functions can be useful in some situations. Putting nonmember functions in a namespace avoids polluting the global namespace.

Nonmember and static member functions may make more sense as members of a new class, especially if they access external resources or have significant dependencies.

Sometimes it is useful to define a function not bound to a class instance. Such a function can be either a static member or a nonmember function. Nonmember functions should not depend on external variables, and should nearly always exist in a namespace. Do not create classes only to group static member functions; this is no different than just giving the function names a common prefix, and such grouping is usually unnecessary anyway.

If you define a nonmember function and it is only needed in its .cc file, use internal linkage to limit its scope.

Local Variables

Place a function's variables in the narrowest scope possible, and initialize variables in the declaration.

C++ allows you to declare variables anywhere in a function. We encourage you to declare them in as local a scope as possible, and as close to the first use as possible. This makes it easier for the reader to find the declaration and see what type the variable is and what it was initialized to. In particular, initialization should be used instead of declaration and assignment, e.g.:

```
int i;
i = f();    // Bad -- initialization separate from declaration.
```

```
int j = g(); // Good -- declaration has initialization.
```

```
std::vector<int> v;
v.push_back(1);  // Prefer initializing using brace initialization.
v.push_back(2);
```

```
std::vector<int> v = {1, 2};  // Good -- v starts initialized.
```

Variables needed for if, while and for statements should normally be declared within those statements, so that such variables are confined to those scopes. E.g.:

```
while (const char* p = strchr(str, '/')) str = p + 1;
```

There is one caveat: if the variable is an object, its constructor is invoked every time it enters scope and is created, and its destructor is invoked every time it goes out of scope.

```
// Inefficient implementation:
for (int i = 0; i < 1000000; ++i) {
  Foo f;  // My ctor and dtor get called 1000000 times each.
  f.DoSomething(i);
}
```

It may be more efficient to declare such a variable used in a loop outside that loop:

```
Foo f;  // My ctor and dtor get called once each.
for (int i = 0; i < 1000000; ++i) {
  f.DoSomething(i);
}
```

Static and Global Variables

Objects with static storage duration are forbidden unless they are trivially destructible. Informally this means that the destructor does not do anything, even taking member and base destructors into account. More formally it means that the type has no user-defined or virtual destructor and that all bases and non-static members are trivially destructible. Static function-local variables may use dynamic initialization. Use of dynamic initialization for static class member variables or variables at namespace scope is discouraged, but allowed in limited circumstances; see below for details.

As a rule of thumb: a global variable satisfies these requirements if its declaration, considered in isolation, could be constexpr.

Every object has a *storage duration*, which correlates with its lifetime. Objects with static storage duration live from the point of their initialization until the end of the program. Such objects appear as variables at namespace scope ("global variables"), as static data members of classes, or as function-local variables that are declared with the static specifier. Function-local static variables are initialized when control first passes through their declaration; all other objects with static storage duration are initialized as part of program start-up. All objects with static storage duration are destroyed at program exit (which happens before unjoined threads are terminated).

Initialization may be *dynamic*, which means that something non-trivial happens during initialization. (For example, consider a constructor that allocates memory, or a variable that is initialized with the current process ID.) The other kind of initialization is *static* initialization. The two aren't quite opposites, though: static initialization *always* happens to objects with static storage duration (initializing the object either to a given constant or to a representation consisting of all bytes set to zero), whereas dynamic initialization happens after that, if required.

Global and static variables are very useful for a large number of applications: named constants, auxiliary data structures internal to some translation unit, command-line flags, logging, registration mechanisms, background infrastructure, etc.

Global and static variables that use dynamic initialization or have non-trivial destructors create complexity that can easily lead to hard-to-find bugs. Dynamic initialization is not ordered across translation units, and neither is destruction (except that destruction happens in reverse order of initialization). When one initialization refers to another variable with static storage duration, it is possible that this causes an object to be accessed before its lifetime has begun (or after its lifetime has ended). Moreover, when a program starts threads that are not joined at exit, those threads may attempt to access objects after their lifetime has ended if their destructor has already run.

Decision on destruction

When destructors are trivial, their execution is not subject to ordering at all (they are effectively not "run"); otherwise we are exposed to the risk of accessing objects after the end of their lifetime. Therefore, we only allow objects with static storage duration if they are trivially destructible. Fundamental types (like pointers and int) are trivially destructible, as are arrays of trivially destructible types. Note that variables marked with constexpr are trivially destructible.

```cpp
const int kNum = 10;  // allowed

struct X { int n; };
const X kX[] = {{1}, {2}, {3}};  // allowed

void foo() {
  static const char* const kMessages[] = {"hello", "world"};  // allowed
}

// allowed: constexpr guarantees trivial destructor
constexpr std::array<int, 3> kArray = {{1, 2, 3}};
```

```cpp
// bad: non-trivial destructor
const std::string kFoo = "foo";

// bad for the same reason, even though kBar is a reference (the
// rule also applies to lifetime-extended temporary objects)
const std::string& kBar = StrCat("a", "b", "c");

void bar() {
  // bad: non-trivial destructor
  static std::map<int, int> kData = {{1, 0}, {2, 0}, {3, 0}};
}
```

Note that references are not objects, and thus they are not subject to the constraints on destructibility. The constraint on dynamic initialization still applies, though. In particular, a function-local static reference of the form static T& t = *new T; is allowed.

Decision on initialization

Initialization is a more complex topic. This is because we must not only consider whether class constructors execute, but we must also consider the evaluation of the initializer:

```
int n = 5;    // fine
int m = f();  // ? (depends on f)
Foo x;        // ? (depends on Foo::Foo)
Bar y = g();  // ? (depends on g and on Bar::Bar)
```

All but the first statement expose us to indeterminate initialization ordering.

The concept we are looking for is called *constant initialization* in the formal language of the C++ standard. It means that the initializing expression is a constant expression, and if the object is initialized by a constructor call, then the constructor must be specified as constexpr , too:

```
struct Foo { constexpr Foo(int) {} };

int n = 5;  // fine, 5 is a constant expression
Foo x(2);   // fine, 2 is a constant expression and the chosen
constructor is constexpr
Foo a[] = { Foo(1), Foo(2), Foo(3) };  // fine
```

Constant initialization is always allowed. Constant initialization of static storage duration variables should be marked
with constexpr or where possible
the ABSL_CONST_INIT attribute. Any non-local static storage duration variable that is not so marked should be presumed to have dynamic initialization, and reviewed very carefully.

By contrast, the following initializations are problematic:

```
// Some declarations used below.
time_t time(time_t*);   // not constexpr!
int f();                // not constexpr!
```

```
struct Bar { Bar() {} };

// Problematic initializations.
time_t m = time(nullptr);  // initializing expression not a constant
                           // expression
Foo y(f());                // ditto
Bar b;                     // chosen constructor Bar::Bar() not constexpr
```

Dynamic initialization of nonlocal variables is discouraged, and in general it is forbidden. However, we do permit it if no aspect of the program depends on the sequencing of this initialization with respect to all other initializations. Under those restrictions, the ordering of the initialization does not make an observable difference. For example:

```
int p = getpid();  // allowed, as long as no other static variable
                   // uses p in its own initialization
```

Dynamic initialization of static local variables is allowed (and common).

Common patterns

- Global strings: if you require a global or static string constant, consider using a simple character array, or a char pointer to the first element of a string literal. String literals have static storage duration already and are usually sufficient.
- Maps, sets, and other dynamic containers: if you require a static, fixed collection, such as a set to search against or a lookup table, you cannot use the dynamic containers from the standard library as a static variable, since they have non-trivial destructors. Instead, consider a simple array of trivial types, e.g. an array of arrays of ints (for a "map from int to int"), or an array of pairs (e.g. pairs of int and const

char*). For small collections, linear search is entirely sufficient (and efficient, due to memory locality); consider using the facilities from absl/algorithm/container.h for the standard operations. If necessary, keep the collection in sorted order and use a binary search algorithm. If you do really prefer a dynamic container from the standard library, consider using a function-local static pointer, as described below.

- Smart pointers (unique_ptr , shared_ptr): smart pointers execute cleanup during destruction and are therefore forbidden. Consider whether your use case fits into one of the other patterns described in this section. One simple solution is to use a plain pointer to a dynamically allocated object and never delete it (see last item).
- Static variables of custom types: if you require static, constant data of a type that you need to define yourself, give the type a trivial destructor and a constexpr constructor.
- If all else fails, you can create an object dynamically and never delete it by using a function-local static pointer or reference (e.g. static const auto& impl = *new T(args...);).

thread_local Variables

thread_local variables that aren't declared inside a function must be initialized with a true compile-time constant, and this must be enforced by using the ABSL_CONST_INIT attribute.

Prefer thread_local over other ways of defining thread-local data.

Starting with C++11, variables can be declared with the thread_local specifier:

```
thread_local Foo foo = ...;
```

Such a variable is actually a collection of objects, so that when different threads access it, they are actually accessing different objects. thread_local variables are much like <u>static storage duration variables</u> in many respects. For instance, they can be declared at namespace scope, inside functions, or as static class members, but not as ordinary class members.

thread_local variable instances are initialized much like static variables, except that they must be initialized separately for each thread, rather than once at program startup. This means that thread_local variables declared within a function are safe, but other thread_local variables are subject to the same initialization-order issues as static variables (and more besides).

thread_local variable instances are destroyed when their thread terminates, so they do not have the destruction-order issues of static variables.

- Thread-local data is inherently safe from races (because only one thread can ordinarily access it), which makes thread_local useful for concurrent programming.
- thread_local is the only standard-supported way of creating thread-local data.
- Accessing a thread_local variable may trigger execution of an unpredictable and uncontrollable amount of other code.
- thread_local variables are effectively global variables, and have all the drawbacks of global variables other than lack of thread-safety.
- The memory consumed by a thread_local variable scales with the number of running threads (in the worst case), which can be quite large in a program.
- An ordinary class member cannot be thread_local.

- thread_local may not be as efficient as certain compiler intrinsics.

thread_local variables inside a function have no safety concerns, so they can be used without restriction. Note that you can use a function-scope thread_local to simulate a class- or namespace-scope thread_local by defining a function or static method that exposes it:

```
Foo& MyThreadLocalFoo() {
  thread_local Foo result = ComplicatedInitialization();
  return result;
}
```

thread_local variables at class or namespace scope must be initialized with a true compile-time constant (i.e. they must have no dynamic initialization). To enforce this, thread_local variables at class or namespace scope must be annotated with ABSL_CONST_INIT (or constexpr, but that should be rare):

```
ABSL_CONST_INIT thread_local Foo foo = ...;
```

thread_local should be preferred over other mechanisms for defining thread-local data.

Classes

Classes are the fundamental unit of code in C++. Naturally, we use them extensively. This section lists the main dos and don'ts you should follow when writing a class.

Doing Work in Constructors

Avoid virtual method calls in constructors, and avoid initialization that can fail if you can't signal an error.

It is possible to perform arbitrary initialization in the body of the constructor.

- No need to worry about whether the class has been initialized or not.
- Objects that are fully initialized by constructor call can be const and may also be easier to use with standard containers or algorithms.

- If the work calls virtual functions, these calls will not get dispatched to the subclass implementations. Future modification to your class can quietly introduce this problem even if your class is not currently subclassed, causing much confusion.
- There is no easy way for constructors to signal errors, short of crashing the program (not always appropriate) or using exceptions (which are <u>forbidden</u>).
- If the work fails, we now have an object whose initialization code failed, so it may be an unusual state requiring a bool IsValid() state checking mechanism (or similar) which is easy to forget to call.
- You cannot take the address of a constructor, so whatever work is done in the constructor cannot easily be handed off to, for example, another thread.

Constructors should never call virtual functions. If appropriate for your code, terminating the program may be an appropriate error handling response. Otherwise, consider a factory function or Init() method as described in <u>TotW #42</u>. Avoid Init() methods on objects with no other states that affect which public methods may be called (semi-constructed objects of this form are particularly hard to work with correctly).

Implicit Conversions

Do not define implicit conversions. Use the `explicit` keyword for conversion operators and single-argument constructors.

Implicit conversions allow an object of one type (called the *source type*) to be used where a different type (called the *destination type*) is expected, such as when passing an `int` argument to a function that takes a `double` parameter.

In addition to the implicit conversions defined by the language, users can define their own, by adding appropriate members to the class definition of the source or destination type. An implicit conversion in the source type is defined by a type conversion operator named after the destination type (e.g. `operator bool()`). An implicit conversion in the destination type is defined by a constructor that can take the source type as its only argument (or only argument with no default value).

The `explicit` keyword can be applied to a constructor or (since C++11) a conversion operator, to ensure that it can only be used when the destination type is explicit at the point of use, e.g. with a cast. This applies not only to implicit conversions, but to C++11's list initialization syntax:

```
class Foo {
  explicit Foo(int x, double y);
  ...
};

void Func(Foo f);
```

```
Func({42, 3.14});  // Error
```

This kind of code isn't technically an implicit conversion, but the language treats it as one as far as `explicit` is concerned.

- Implicit conversions can make a type more usable and expressive by eliminating the need to explicitly name a type when it's obvious.

- Implicit conversions can be a simpler alternative to overloading, such as when a single function with a `string_view` parameter takes the place of separate overloads for `std::string` and `const char*`.
- List initialization syntax is a concise and expressive way of initializing objects.

- Implicit conversions can hide type-mismatch bugs, where the destination type does not match the user's expectation, or the user is unaware that any conversion will take place.
- Implicit conversions can make code harder to read, particularly in the presence of overloading, by making it less obvious what code is actually getting called.
- Constructors that take a single argument may accidentally be usable as implicit type conversions, even if they are not intended to do so.
- When a single-argument constructor is not marked `explicit`, there's no reliable way to tell whether it's intended to define an implicit conversion, or the author simply forgot to mark it.
- It's not always clear which type should provide the conversion, and if they both do, the code becomes ambiguous.
- List initialization can suffer from the same problems if the destination type is implicit, particularly if the list has only a single element.

Type conversion operators, and constructors that are callable with a single argument, must be marked `explicit` in the class definition. As an exception, copy and move constructors should not be `explicit`, since they do not perform type conversion. Implicit conversions can sometimes be necessary and appropriate for types that are designed to transparently wrap other types. In that case, contact your project leads to request a waiver of this rule.

Constructors that cannot be called with a single argument may omit `explicit`. Constructors that take a single `std::initializer_list` parameter should also omit `explicit`, in order to support copy-initialization (e.g. `MyType m = {1, 2};`).

Copyable and Movable Types

A class's public API must make clear whether the class is copyable, move-only, or neither copyable nor movable. Support copying and/or moving if these operations are clear and meaningful for your type.

A movable type is one that can be initialized and assigned from temporaries.

A copyable type is one that can be initialized or assigned from any other object of the same type (so is also movable by definition), with the stipulation that the value of the source does not change. `std::unique_ptr<int>` is an example of a movable but not copyable type (since the value of the source `std::unique_ptr<int>` must be modified during assignment to the destination). `int` and `std::string` are examples of movable types that are also copyable. (For `int`, the move and copy operations are the same; for `std::string`, there exists a move operation that is less expensive than a copy.)

For user-defined types, the copy behavior is defined by the copy constructor and the copy-assignment operator. Move behavior is defined by the move constructor and the move-assignment operator, if they exist, or by the copy constructor and the copy-assignment operator otherwise.

The copy/move constructors can be implicitly invoked by the compiler in some situations, e.g. when passing objects by value.

Objects of copyable and movable types can be passed and returned by value, which makes APIs simpler, safer, and more general. Unlike when passing objects by pointer or reference, there's no risk of confusion over ownership, lifetime, mutability, and similar issues, and no need to specify them in the contract. It also prevents non-local interactions between the client and the implementation, which makes them easier to understand, maintain, and optimize by the compiler. Further, such objects can be used with generic APIs that require pass-by-value, such as most containers, and they allow for additional flexibility in e.g., type composition.

Copy/move constructors and assignment operators are usually easier to define correctly than alternatives like Clone() , CopyFrom() or Swap() , because they can be generated by the compiler, either implicitly or with = default . They are concise, and ensure that all data members are copied. Copy and move constructors are also generally more efficient, because they don't require heap allocation or separate initialization and assignment steps, and they're eligible for optimizations such as copy elision.

Move operations allow the implicit and efficient transfer of resources out of rvalue objects. This allows a plainer coding style in some cases.

Some types do not need to be copyable, and providing copy operations for such types can be confusing, nonsensical, or outright incorrect. Types representing singleton objects (Registerer), objects tied to a specific scope (Cleanup), or closely coupled to object identity (Mutex) cannot be copied meaningfully. Copy operations for base class types that are to be used polymorphically are hazardous, because use of them can lead to object slicing. Defaulted or carelessly-implemented copy operations can be incorrect, and the resulting bugs can be confusing and difficult to diagnose.

Copy constructors are invoked implicitly, which makes the invocation easy to miss. This may cause confusion for programmers used to languages where pass-by-reference is conventional or mandatory. It may also encourage excessive copying, which can cause performance problems.

Every class's public interface must make clear which copy and move operations the class supports. This should usually take the form of explicitly declaring and/or deleting the appropriate operations in the public section of the declaration.

Specifically, a copyable class should explicitly declare the copy operations, a move-only class should explicitly declare the move operations, and a non-copyable/movable class should explicitly delete the copy operations. Explicitly declaring or deleting all four copy/move operations is permitted, but not required. If you provide a copy or move assignment operator, you must also provide the corresponding constructor.

```cpp
class Copyable {
public:
  Copyable(const Copyable& other) = default;
  Copyable& operator=(const Copyable& other) = default;

  // The implicit move operations are suppressed by the declarations above.
};

class MoveOnly {
public:
  MoveOnly(MoveOnly&& other);
  MoveOnly& operator=(MoveOnly&& other);

  // The copy operations are implicitly deleted, but you can
  // spell that out explicitly if you want:
  MoveOnly(const MoveOnly&) = delete;
  MoveOnly& operator=(const MoveOnly&) = delete;
};
```

```cpp
class NotCopyableOrMovable {
public:
  // Not copyable or movable
  NotCopyableOrMovable(const NotCopyableOrMovable&) = delete;
  NotCopyableOrMovable& operator=(const NotCopyableOrMovable&)
      = delete;

  // The move operations are implicitly disabled, but you can
  // spell that out explicitly if you want:
  NotCopyableOrMovable(NotCopyableOrMovable&&) = delete;
  NotCopyableOrMovable& operator=(NotCopyableOrMovable&&)
      = delete;
};
```

These declarations/deletions can be omitted only if they are obvious:
- If the class has no private section, like a struct or an interface-only base class, then the copyability/movability can be determined by the copyability/movability of any public data members.
- If a base class clearly isn't copyable or movable, derived classes naturally won't be either. An interface-only base class that leaves these operations implicit is not sufficient to make concrete subclasses clear.
- Note that if you explicitly declare or delete either the constructor or assignment operation for copy, the other copy operation is not obvious and must be declared or deleted. Likewise for move operations.

A type should not be copyable/movable if the meaning of copying/moving is unclear to a casual user, or if it incurs unexpected costs. Move operations for copyable types are strictly a performance optimization and are a potential source of bugs and complexity, so avoid defining them unless they are significantly more efficient than the corresponding copy operations. If your type provides copy operations, it is recommended that you design your class so that the default implementation of those operations is correct. Remember to review the correctness of any defaulted operations as you would any other code.

Due to the risk of slicing, prefer to avoid providing a public assignment operator or copy/move constructor for a class that's intended to be derived from (and prefer to avoid deriving from a class with such members). If your base class needs to be copyable, provide a public virtual Clone() method, and a protected copy constructor that derived classes can use to implement it.

Structs vs. Classes

Use a struct only for passive objects that carry data; everything else is a class .

The struct and class keywords behave almost identically in C++. We add our own semantic meanings to each keyword, so you should use the appropriate keyword for the data-type you're defining.

structs should be used for passive objects that carry data, and may have associated constants, but lack any functionality other than access/setting the data members. All fields must be public, and accessed directly rather than through getter/setter methods. The struct must not have invariants that imply relationships between different fields, since direct user access to those fields may break those invariants. Methods should not provide behavior but should only be used to set up the data members, e.g., constructor, destructor, Initialize() , Reset() .

If more functionality or invariants are required, a class is more appropriate. If in doubt, make it a class.

For consistency with STL, you can use struct instead of class for stateless types, such as traits, template metafunctions, and some functors.

Note that member variables in structs and classes have different naming rules.

Structs vs. Pairs and Tuples

Prefer to use a struct instead of a pair or a tuple whenever the elements can have meaningful names.

While using pairs and tuples can avoid the need to define a custom type, potentially saving work when *writing* code, a meaningful field name will almost always be much clearer when *reading* code than .first, .second, or std::get<X>. While C++14's introduction of std::get<Type> to access a tuple element by type rather than index (when the type is unique) can sometimes partially mitigate this, a field name is usually substantially clearer and more informative than a type.

Pairs and tuples may be appropriate in generic code where there are not specific meanings for the elements of the pair or tuple. Their use may also be required in order to interoperate with existing code or APIs.

Inheritance

Composition is often more appropriate than inheritance. When using inheritance, make it public.

When a sub-class inherits from a base class, it includes the definitions of all the data and operations that the base class defines. "Interface inheritance" is inheritance from a pure abstract base class (one with no state or defined methods); all other inheritance is "implementation inheritance".

Implementation inheritance reduces code size by re-using the base class code as it specializes an existing type. Because inheritance is a compile-time declaration, you and the compiler can understand the operation and detect errors. Interface inheritance can be used to programmatically enforce that a class expose a particular API. Again, the compiler can detect errors, in this case, when a class does not define a necessary method of the API.

For implementation inheritance, because the code implementing a sub-class is spread between the base and the sub-class, it can be more difficult to understand an implementation. The sub-class cannot override functions that are not virtual, so the sub-class cannot change implementation.

Multiple inheritance is especially problematic, because it often imposes a higher performance overhead (in fact, the performance drop from single inheritance to multiple inheritance can often be greater than the performance drop from ordinary to virtual dispatch), and because it risks leading to "diamond" inheritance patterns, which are prone to ambiguity, confusion, and outright bugs.

All inheritance should be public . If you want to do private inheritance, you should be including an instance of the base class as a member instead.

Do not overuse implementation inheritance. Composition is often more appropriate. Try to restrict use of inheritance to the "is-a" case: Bar subclasses Foo if it can reasonably be said that Bar "is a kind of" Foo .

Limit the use of protected to those member functions that might need to be accessed from subclasses. Note that <u>data members should be private</u>.

Explicitly annotate overrides of virtual functions or virtual destructors with exactly one of an override or (less frequently) final specifier. Do not use virtual when declaring an override. Rationale: A function or destructor marked override or final that is not an override of a base class virtual function will not compile, and this helps catch common errors. The specifiers serve as documentation; if no specifier is present, the reader has to check all ancestors of the class in question to determine if the function or destructor is virtual or not.

Multiple inheritance is permitted, but
multiple *implementation* inheritance is strongly discouraged.

Operator Overloading

Overload operators judiciously. Do not use user-defined literals.

C++ permits user code to declare overloaded versions of the built-in operators using the operator keyword, so long as one of the parameters is a user-defined type. The operator keyword also permits user code to define new kinds of literals using operator"" , and to define type-conversion functions such as operator bool() .

Operator overloading can make code more concise and intuitive by enabling user-defined types to behave the same as built-in types. Overloaded operators are the idiomatic names for certain operations (e.g. == , < , = , and <<), and adhering to those conventions can make user-defined types more readable and enable them to interoperate with libraries that expect those names.

User-defined literals are a very concise notation for creating objects of user-defined types.

- Providing a correct, consistent, and unsurprising set of operator overloads requires some care, and failure to do so can lead to confusion and bugs.
- Overuse of operators can lead to obfuscated code, particularly if the overloaded operator's semantics don't follow convention.
- The hazards of function overloading apply just as much to operator overloading, if not more so.

- Operator overloads can fool our intuition into thinking that expensive operations are cheap, built-in operations.
- Finding the call sites for overloaded operators may require a search tool that's aware of C++ syntax, rather than e.g. grep.
- If you get the argument type of an overloaded operator wrong, you may get a different overload rather than a compiler error. For example, foo < bar may do one thing, while &foo < &bar does something totally different.
- Certain operator overloads are inherently hazardous. Overloading unary & can cause the same code to have different meanings depending on whether the overload declaration is visible. Overloads of && , || , and , (comma) cannot match the evaluation-order semantics of the built-in operators.
- Operators are often defined outside the class, so there's a risk of different files introducing different definitions of the same operator. If both definitions are linked into the same binary, this results in undefined behavior, which can manifest as subtle run-time bugs.
- User-defined literals (UDLs) allow the creation of new syntactic forms that are unfamiliar even to experienced C++ programmers, such as "Hello World"sv as a shorthand for std::string_view("Hello World") . Existing notations are clearer, though less terse.
- Because they can't be namespace-qualified, uses of UDLs also require use of either using-directives (which we ban) or using-declarations (which we ban in header files except when the imported names are part of the interface exposed by the header file in question). Given that header files would have to avoid UDL suffixes, we prefer to avoid

having conventions for literals differ between header files and source files.

Define overloaded operators only if their meaning is obvious, unsurprising, and consistent with the corresponding built-in operators. For example, use `|` as a bitwise- or logical-or, not as a shell-style pipe.

Define operators only on your own types. More precisely, define them in the same headers, .cc files, and namespaces as the types they operate on. That way, the operators are available wherever the type is, minimizing the risk of multiple definitions. If possible, avoid defining operators as templates, because they must satisfy this rule for any possible template arguments. If you define an operator, also define any related operators that make sense, and make sure they are defined consistently. For example, if you overload `<`, overload all the comparison operators, and make sure `<` and `>` never return true for the same arguments.

Prefer to define non-modifying binary operators as non-member functions. If a binary operator is defined as a class member, implicit conversions will apply to the right-hand argument, but not the left-hand one. It will confuse your users if `a < b` compiles but `b < a` doesn't.

Don't go out of your way to avoid defining operator overloads. For example, prefer to define `==`, `=`, and `<<`, rather than `Equals()`, `CopyFrom()`, and `PrintTo()`. Conversely, don't define operator overloads just because other libraries expect them. For example, if your type doesn't have a natural ordering, but you want to store it in a `std::set`, use a custom comparator rather than overloading `<`.

Do not overload `&&`, `||`, `,` (comma), or unary `&`. Do not overload `operator""`, i.e. do not introduce user-defined literals. Do not use any such literals provided by others (including the standard library).

Type conversion operators are covered in the section on implicit conversions. The = operator is covered in the section on copy constructors. Overloading << for use with streams is covered in the section on streams. See also the rules on function overloading, which apply to operator overloading as well.

Access Control

Make classes' data members private , unless they are constants. This simplifies reasoning about invariants, at the cost of some easy boilerplate in the form of accessors (usually const) if necessary.

For technical reasons, we allow data members of a test fixture class in a .cc file to be protected when using Test).

Declaration Order

Group similar declarations together, placing public parts earlier.

A class definition should usually start with a public: section, followed by protected: , then private: . Omit sections that would be empty.

Within each section, generally prefer grouping similar kinds of declarations together, and generally prefer the following order: types (including typedef , using , and nested structs and classes), constants, factory functions, constructors, assignment operators, destructor, all other methods, data members.

Do not put large method definitions inline in the class definition. Usually, only trivial or performance-critical, and very short, methods may be defined inline. See Inline Functions for more details.

Functions

Output Parameters

The output of a C++ function is naturally provided via a return value and sometimes via output parameters.

Prefer using return values over output parameters: they improve readability, and often provide the same or better performance. If output-only parameters are used, they should appear after input parameters.

Parameters are either input to the function, output from the function, or both. Input parameters are usually values or const references, while output and input/output parameters will be pointers to non-const .

When ordering function parameters, put all input-only parameters before any output parameters. In particular, do not add new parameters to the end of the function just because they are new; place new input-only parameters before the output parameters.

This is not a hard-and-fast rule. Parameters that are both input and output (often classes/structs) muddy the waters, and, as always, consistency with related functions may require you to bend the rule.

Write Short Functions

Prefer small and focused functions.

We recognize that long functions are sometimes appropriate, so no hard limit is placed on functions length. If a function exceeds about 40 lines, think about whether it can be broken up without harming the structure of the program.

Even if your long function works perfectly now, someone modifying it in a few months may add new behavior. This could result in bugs that are hard to find. Keeping your functions short and simple makes it easier for other people to read and modify your code. Small functions are also easier to test.

You could find long and complicated functions when working with some code. Do not be intimidated by modifying existing code: if working with such a function proves to be difficult, you find that errors are hard to debug, or you want to use a piece of it in several different contexts, consider breaking up the function into smaller and more manageable pieces.

Reference Arguments

All parameters passed by lvalue reference must be labeled `const`.

In C, if a function needs to modify a variable, the parameter must use a pointer, eg `int foo(int *pval)`. In C++, the function can alternatively declare a reference parameter: `int foo(int &val)`.

Defining a parameter as reference avoids ugly code like `(*pval)++`. Necessary for some applications like copy constructors. Makes it clear, unlike with pointers, that a null pointer is not a possible value.

References can be confusing, as they have value syntax but pointer semantics.

Within function parameter lists all references must be `const`:

```
void Foo(const std::string &in, std::string *out);
```

In fact it is a very strong convention in code that input arguments are values or `const` references while output arguments are pointers. Input parameters may be `const` pointers, but we never allow non-`const` reference parameters except when required by convention, e.g., `swap()`.

However, there are some instances where using `const T*` is preferable to `const T&` for input parameters. For example:
- You want to pass in a null pointer.
- The function saves a pointer or reference to the input.

Remember that most of the time input parameters are going to be specified as `const T&`. Using `const T*` instead communicates to the reader that the input is somehow treated differently. So if you choose `const T*` rather than `const T&`, do so for a concrete reason; otherwise it will likely confuse readers by making them look for an explanation that doesn't exist.

Function Overloading

Use overloaded functions (including constructors) only if a reader looking at a call site can get a good idea of what is happening without having to first figure out exactly which overload is being called.

You may write a function that takes a const std::string& and overload it with another that takes const char* . However, in this case consider std::string_view instead.

```
class MyClass {
public:
  void Analyze(const std::string &text);
  void Analyze(const char *text, size_t textlen);
};
```

Overloading can make code more intuitive by allowing an identically-named function to take different arguments. It may be necessary for templatized code, and it can be convenient for Visitors.

Overloading based on const or ref qualification may make utility code more usable, more efficient, or both. (See TotW 148 for more.)

If a function is overloaded by the argument types alone, a reader may have to understand C++'s complex matching rules in order to tell what's going on. Also many people are confused by the semantics of inheritance if a derived class overrides only some of the variants of a function.

You may overload a function when there are no semantic differences between variants. These overloads may vary in types, qualifiers, or argument count. However, a reader of such a call must not need to know which member of the overload set is chosen, only that **something** from the set is being called. If you can document all entries in the overload set with a single comment in the header, that is a good sign that it is a well-designed overload set.

Default Arguments

Default arguments are allowed on non-virtual functions when the default is guaranteed to always have the same value. Follow the same restrictions as for function overloading, and prefer overloaded functions if the readability gained with default arguments doesn't outweigh the downsides below.

Often you have a function that uses default values, but occasionally you want to override the defaults. Default parameters allow an easy way to do this without having to define many functions for the rare exceptions. Compared to overloading the function, default arguments have a cleaner syntax, with less boilerplate and a clearer distinction between 'required' and 'optional' arguments.

Defaulted arguments are another way to achieve the semantics of overloaded functions, so all the reasons not to overload functions apply.

The defaults for arguments in a virtual function call are determined by the static type of the target object, and there's no guarantee that all overrides of a given function declare the same defaults.

Default parameters are re-evaluated at each call site, which can bloat the generated code. Readers may also expect the default's value to be fixed at the declaration instead of varying at each call.

Function pointers are confusing in the presence of default arguments, since the function signature often doesn't match the call signature. Adding function overloads avoids these problems.

Default arguments are banned on virtual functions, where they don't work properly, and in cases where the specified default might not evaluate to the same value depending on when it was evaluated. (For example, don't write void f(int n = counter++); .)

In some other cases, default arguments can improve the readability of their function declarations enough to overcome the downsides above, so they are allowed. When in doubt, use overloads.

Trailing Return Type Syntax

Use trailing return types only where using the ordinary syntax (leading return types) is impractical or much less readable.

C++ allows two different forms of function declarations. In the older form, the return type appears before the function name. For example:

```
int foo(int x);
```

The newer form, introduced in C++11, uses the auto keyword before the function name and a trailing return type after the argument list. For example, the declaration above could equivalently be written:

```
auto foo(int x) -> int;
```

The trailing return type is in the function's scope. This doesn't make a difference for a simple case like int but it matters for more complicated cases, like types declared in class scope or types written in terms of the function parameters.

Trailing return types are the only way to explicitly specify the return type of a lambda expression. In some cases the compiler is able to deduce a lambda's return type, but not in all cases. Even when the compiler can deduce it automatically, sometimes specifying it explicitly would be clearer for readers.

Sometimes it's easier and more readable to specify a return type after the function's parameter list has already appeared. This is particularly true when the return type depends on template parameters. For example:

```
template <typename T, typename U>
auto add(T t, U u) -> decltype(t + u);
```

versus

```
template <typename T, typename U>
decltype(declval<T&>() + declval<U&>()) add(T t, U u);
```

Trailing return type syntax is relatively new and it has no analogue in C++-like languages such as C and Java, so some readers may find it unfamiliar.

Existing code bases have an enormous number of function declarations that aren't going to get changed to use the new syntax, so the realistic choices are using the old syntax only or using a mixture of the two. Using a single version is better for uniformity of style.

In most cases, continue to use the older style of function declaration where the return type goes before the function name. Use the new trailing-return-type form only in cases where it's required (such as lambdas) or where, by putting the type after the function's parameter list, it allows you to write the type in a much more readable way. The latter case should be rare; it's mostly an issue in fairly complicated template code, which is discouraged in most cases.

There are various tricks and utilities that we use to make C++ code more robust, and various ways we use C++ that may differ from what you see elsewhere.

Ownership and Smart Pointers

Prefer to have single, fixed owners for dynamically allocated objects. Prefer to transfer ownership with smart pointers.

"Ownership" is a bookkeeping technique for managing dynamically allocated memory (and other resources). The owner of a dynamically allocated object is an object or function that is responsible for ensuring that it is deleted when no longer needed. Ownership can sometimes be shared, in which case the last owner is typically responsible for deleting it. Even when ownership is not shared, it can be transferred from one piece of code to another.

"Smart" pointers are classes that act like pointers, e.g. by overloading the * and -> operators. Some smart pointer types can be used to automate ownership bookkeeping, to ensure these responsibilities are met. std::unique_ptr is a smart pointer type introduced in C++11, which expresses exclusive ownership of a dynamically allocated object; the object is deleted when the std::unique_ptr goes out of scope. It cannot be copied, but can be *moved* to represent ownership transfer. std::shared_ptr is a smart pointer type that expresses shared ownership of a dynamically allocated object. std::shared_ptr s can be copied; ownership of the object is shared among all copies, and the object is deleted when the last std::shared_ptr is destroyed.

- It's virtually impossible to manage dynamically allocated memory without some sort of ownership logic.
- Transferring ownership of an object can be cheaper than copying it (if copying it is even possible).
- Transferring ownership can be simpler than 'borrowing' a pointer or reference, because it reduces the need to coordinate the lifetime of the object between the two users.
- Smart pointers can improve readability by making ownership logic explicit, self-documenting, and unambiguous.
- Smart pointers can eliminate manual ownership bookkeeping, simplifying the code and ruling out large classes of errors.

- For const objects, shared ownership can be a simple and efficient alternative to deep copying.

- Ownership must be represented and transferred via pointers (whether smart or plain). Pointer semantics are more complicated than value semantics, especially in APIs: you have to worry not just about ownership, but also aliasing, lifetime, and mutability, among other issues.

- The performance costs of value semantics are often overestimated, so the performance benefits of ownership transfer might not justify the readability and complexity costs.

- APIs that transfer ownership force their clients into a single memory management model.

- Code using smart pointers is less explicit about where the resource releases take place.

- std::unique_ptr expresses ownership transfer using C++11's move semantics, which are relatively new and may confuse some programmers.

- Shared ownership can be a tempting alternative to careful ownership design, obfuscating the design of a system.

- Shared ownership requires explicit bookkeeping at run-time, which can be costly.

- In some cases (e.g. cyclic references), objects with shared ownership may never be deleted.

- Smart pointers are not perfect substitutes for plain pointers.

If dynamic allocation is necessary, prefer to keep ownership with the code that allocated it. If other code needs access to the object, consider passing it a copy, or passing a pointer or reference without transferring ownership. Prefer to use std::unique_ptr to make ownership transfer explicit. For example:

```
std::unique_ptr<Foo> FooFactory();
void FooConsumer(std::unique_ptr<Foo> ptr);
```

Do not design your code to use shared ownership without a very good reason. One such reason is to avoid expensive copy operations, but you should only do this if the performance benefits are significant, and the underlying object is immutable (i.e. std::shared_ptr<const Foo>). If you do use shared ownership, prefer to use std::shared_ptr .

Never use std::auto_ptr . Instead, use std::unique_ptr .

cpplint

Use cpplint.py to detect style errors.

cpplint.py is a tool that reads a source file and identifies many style errors. It is not perfect, and has both false positives and false negatives, but it is still a valuable tool. False positives can be ignored by putting // NOLINT at the end of the line or // NOLINTNEXTLINE in the previous line.

Some projects have instructions on how to run cpplint.py from their project tools. If the project you are contributing to does not, you can download cpplint.py separately.

Other C++ Features

Rvalue References

Use rvalue references to:
- Define move constructors and move assignment operators.

- Define <u>overload sets</u> with const& and && variants if you have evidence that this provides meaningfully better performance than passing by value, or if you're writing low-overhead generic code that needs to support arbitrary types. Beware combinatorial overload sets, that is, seldom overload more than one parameter.
- Support 'perfect forwarding' in generic code.

Rvalue references are a type of reference that can only bind to temporary objects. The syntax is similar to traditional reference syntax. For example, void f(std::string&& s); declares a function whose argument is an rvalue reference to a std::string.

When the token '&&' is applied to an unqualified template argument in a function parameter, special template argument deduction rules apply. Such a reference is called forwarding reference.

- Defining a move constructor (a constructor taking an rvalue reference to the class type) makes it possible to move a value instead of copying it. If v1 is a std::vector<std::string>, for example, then auto v2(std::move(v1)) will probably just result in some simple pointer manipulation instead of copying a large amount of data. In many cases this can result in a major performance improvement.
- Rvalue references make it possible to implement types that are movable but not copyable, which can be useful for types that have no sensible definition of copying but where you might still want to pass them as function arguments, put them in containers, etc.
- std::move is necessary to make effective use of some standard-library types, such as std::unique_ptr.
- <u>Forwarding references</u> which use the rvalue reference token, make it possible to write a generic function wrapper

that forwards its arguments to another function, and works whether or not its arguments are temporary objects and/or const. This is called 'perfect forwarding'.

- Rvalue references are not yet widely understood. Rules like reference collapsing and the special deduction rule for forwarding references are somewhat obscure.
- Rvalue references are often misused. Using rvalue references is counter-intuitive in signatures where the argument is expected to have a valid specified state after the function call, or where no move operation is performed.

You may use rvalue references to define move constructors and move assignment operators (as described in Copyable and Movable Types). See the C++ Primer for more information about move semantics and `std::move`.

You may use rvalue references to define pairs of overloads, one taking `Foo&&` and the other taking `const Foo&`. Usually the preferred solution is just to pass by value, but an overloaded pair of functions sometimes yields better performance and is sometimes necessary in generic code that needs to support a wide variety of types. As always: if you're writing more complicated code for the sake of performance, make sure you have evidence that it actually helps.

You may use forwarding references in conjunction with `std::forward`, to support perfect forwarding.

Friends

We allow use of `friend` classes and functions, within reason.

Friends should usually be defined in the same file so that the reader does not have to look in another file to find uses of the private members of a class. A common use of `friend` is to have a FooBuilder class be a friend of Foo so that it can construct the inner state of Foo correctly, without exposing this state to the world. In some cases it may be useful to make a unittest class a friend of the class it tests.

Friends extend, but do not break, the encapsulation boundary of a class. In some cases this is better than making a member public when you want to give only one other class access to it. However, most classes should interact with other classes solely through their public members.

Exceptions

We do not use C++ exceptions.

- Exceptions allow higher levels of an application to decide how to handle "can't happen" failures in deeply nested functions, without the obscuring and error-prone bookkeeping of error codes.
- Exceptions are used by most other modern languages. Using them in C++ would make it more consistent with Python, Java, and the C++ that others are familiar with.
- Some third-party C++ libraries use exceptions, and turning them off internally makes it harder to integrate with those libraries.
- Exceptions are the only way for a constructor to fail. We can simulate this with a factory function or an Init() method, but these require heap allocation or a new "invalid" state, respectively.
- Exceptions are really handy in testing frameworks.

- When you add a throw statement to an existing function, you must examine all of its transitive callers. Either they must make at least the basic exception safety guarantee, or they must never catch the exception and be happy with

the program terminating as a result. For instance, if f() calls g() calls h(), and h throws an exception that f catches, g has to be careful or it may not clean up properly.
- More generally, exceptions make the control flow of programs difficult to evaluate by looking at code: functions may return in places you don't expect. This causes maintainability and debugging difficulties. You can minimize this cost via some rules on how and where exceptions can be used, but at the cost of more that a developer needs to know and understand.
- Exception safety requires both RAII and different coding practices. Lots of supporting machinery is needed to make writing correct exception-safe code easy. Further, to avoid requiring readers to understand the entire call graph, exception-safe code must isolate logic that writes to persistent state into a "commit" phase. This will have both benefits and costs (perhaps where you're forced to obfuscate code to isolate the commit). Allowing exceptions would force us to always pay those costs even when they're not worth it.
- Turning on exceptions adds data to each binary produced, increasing compile time (probably slightly) and possibly increasing address space pressure.
- The availability of exceptions may encourage developers to throw them when they are not appropriate or recover from them when it's not safe to do so. For example, invalid user input should not cause exceptions to be thrown. We would need to make the style guide even longer to document these restrictions!

On their face, the benefits of using exceptions outweigh the costs, especially in new projects. However, for existing code, the introduction of exceptions has implications on all dependent code. If exceptions can be propagated beyond a new project, it also becomes problematic to integrate the new project into existing exception-free code. Because most existing C++ code is not prepared to deal with exceptions, it is comparatively difficult to adopt new code that generates exceptions.

Given that existing code is not exception-tolerant, the costs of using exceptions are somewhat greater than the costs in a new project. The conversion process would be slow and error-prone. We don't believe that the available alternatives to exceptions, such as error codes and assertions, introduce a significant burden.

Our advice against using exceptions is not predicated on philosophical or moral grounds, but practical ones. Because we'd like to use our open-source projects and it's difficult to do so if those projects use exceptions, we need to advise against exceptions in open-source projects as well. Things would probably be different if we had to do it all over again from scratch.

This prohibition also applies to the exception handling related features added in C++11, such as std::exception_ptr and std::nested_exception .

There is an exception to this rule (no pun intended) for Windows code.

noexcept

Specify noexcept when it is useful and correct.

The noexcept specifier is used to specify whether a function will throw exceptions or not. If an exception escapes from a function marked noexcept , the program crashes via std::terminate .

The noexcept operator performs a compile-time check that returns true if an expression is declared to not throw any exceptions.

- Specifying move constructors as noexcept improves performance in some cases,

- e.g. std::vector<T>::resize() moves rather than copies the objects if T's move constructor is noexcept.
- Specifying noexcept on a function can trigger compiler optimizations in environments where exceptions are enabled, e.g. compiler does not have to generate extra code for stack-unwinding, if it knows that no exceptions can be thrown due to a noexcept specifier.
- In projects following this guide that have exceptions disabled it is hard to ensure that noexcept specifiers are correct, and hard to define what correctness even means.
- It's hard, if not impossible, to undo noexcept because it eliminates a guarantee that callers may be relying on, in ways that are hard to detect.

You may use noexcept when it is useful for performance if it accurately reflects the intended semantics of your function, i.e. that if an exception is somehow thrown from within the function body then it represents a fatal error. You can assume that noexcept on move constructors has a meaningful performance benefit. If you think there is significant performance benefit from
specifying noexcept on some other function, please discuss it with your project leads.

Prefer unconditional noexcept if exceptions are completely disabled (i.e. most C++ environments). Otherwise, use
conditional noexcept specifiers with simple conditions, in ways that evaluate false only in the few cases where the function could potentially throw. The tests might include type traits check on whether the involved operation might throw
(e.g. std::is_nothrow_move_constructible for move-constructing objects), or on whether allocation can throw
(e.g. absl::default_allocator_is_nothrow for standard default allocation). Note in many cases the only possible cause for an

exception is allocation failure (we believe move constructors should not throw except due to allocation failure), and there are many applications where it's appropriate to treat memory exhaustion as a fatal error rather than an exceptional condition that your program should attempt to recover from. Even for other potential failures you should prioritize interface simplicity over supporting all possible exception throwing scenarios: instead of writing a complicated `noexcept` clause that depends on whether a hash function can throw, for example, simply document that your component doesn't support hash functions throwing and make it unconditionally `noexcept`.

Run-Time Type Information (RTTI)

Avoid using Run Time Type Information (RTTI).

RTTI allows a programmer to query the C++ class of an object at run time. This is done by use of `typeid` or `dynamic_cast`.

The standard alternatives to RTTI (described below) require modification or redesign of the class hierarchy in question. Sometimes such modifications are infeasible or undesirable, particularly in widely-used or mature code.

RTTI can be useful in some unit tests. For example, it is useful in tests of factory classes where the test has to verify that a newly created object has the expected dynamic type. It is also useful in managing the relationship between objects and their mocks.

RTTI is useful when considering multiple abstract objects. Consider

```cpp
bool Base::Equal(Base* other) = 0;
bool Derived::Equal(Base* other) {
  Derived* that = dynamic_cast<Derived*>(other);
  if (that == nullptr)
    return false;
  ...
}
```

Querying the type of an object at run-time frequently means a design problem. Needing to know the type of an object at runtime is often an indication that the design of your class hierarchy is flawed.

Undisciplined use of RTTI makes code hard to maintain. It can lead to type-based decision trees or switch statements scattered throughout the code, all of which must be examined when making further changes.

RTTI has legitimate uses but is prone to abuse, so you must be careful when using it. You may use it freely in unittests, but avoid it when possible in other code. In particular, think twice before using RTTI in new code. If you find yourself needing to write code that behaves differently based on the class of an object, consider one of the following alternatives to querying the type:

- Virtual methods are the preferred way of executing different code paths depending on a specific subclass type. This puts the work within the object itself.
- If the work belongs outside the object and instead in some processing code, consider a double-dispatch solution, such as the Visitor design pattern. This allows a facility outside the object itself to determine the type of class using the built-in type system.

When the logic of a program guarantees that a given instance of a base class is in fact an instance of a particular derived class, then a dynamic_cast may be used freely on the object. Usually one can use a static_cast as an alternative in such situations.

Decision trees based on type are a strong indication that your code is on the wrong track.

```
if (typeid(*data) == typeid(D1)) {
   ...
} else if (typeid(*data) == typeid(D2)) {
```

```
...
} else if (typeid(*data) == typeid(D3)) {
...
```

Code such as this usually breaks when additional subclasses are added to the class hierarchy. Moreover, when properties of a subclass change, it is difficult to find and modify all the affected code segments.

Do not hand-implement an RTTI-like workaround. The arguments against RTTI apply just as much to workarounds like class hierarchies with type tags. Moreover, workarounds disguise your true intent.

Casting

Use C++-style casts like static_cast<float>(double_value) , or brace initialization for conversion of arithmetic types like int64 y = int64{1} << 42 . Do not use cast formats like int y = (int)x or int y = int(x) (but the latter is okay when invoking a constructor of a class type).

C++ introduced a different cast system from C that distinguishes the types of cast operations.

The problem with C casts is the ambiguity of the operation; sometimes you are doing a *conversion* (e.g., (int)3.5) and sometimes you are doing a *cast* (e.g., (int)"hello"). Brace initialization and C++ casts can often help avoid this ambiguity. Additionally, C++ casts are more visible when searching for them.

The C++-style cast syntax is verbose and cumbersome.

Do not use C-style casts. Instead, use these C++-style casts when explicit type conversion is necessary.

- Use brace initialization to convert arithmetic types (e.g. int64{x}). This is the safest approach because code

will not compile if conversion can result in information loss. The syntax is also concise.
- Use static_cast as the equivalent of a C-style cast that does value conversion, when you need to explicitly up-cast a pointer from a class to its superclass, or when you need to explicitly cast a pointer from a superclass to a subclass. In this last case, you must be sure your object is actually an instance of the subclass.
- Use const_cast to remove the const qualifier (see const).
- Use reinterpret_cast to do unsafe conversions of pointer types to and from integer and other pointer types. Use this only if you know what you are doing and you understand the aliasing issues. Also, consider the alternative absl::bit_cast.
- Use absl::bit_cast to interpret the raw bits of a value using a different type of the same size (a type pun), such as interpreting the bits of a double as int64.

See the RTTI section for guidance on the use of dynamic_cast.

Streams

Use streams where appropriate, and stick to "simple" usages. Overload << for streaming only for types representing values, and write only the user-visible value, not any implementation details.

Streams are the standard I/O abstraction in C++, as exemplified by the standard header <iostream>. They are widely used in code, mostly for debug logging and test diagnostics.

The << and >> stream operators provide an API for formatted I/O that is easily learned, portable, reusable, and extensible. printf, by contrast, doesn't even support std::string, to say nothing of user-defined types, and is very difficult to use portably. printf also obliges you to choose among the numerous slightly different versions of that function, and navigate the dozens of conversion specifiers.

Streams provide first-class support for console I/O via `std::cin`, `std::cout`, `std::cerr`, and `std::clog`. The C APIs do as well, but are hampered by the need to manually buffer the input.

- Stream formatting can be configured by mutating the state of the stream. Such mutations are persistent, so the behavior of your code can be affected by the entire previous history of the stream, unless you go out of your way to restore it to a known state every time other code might have touched it. User code can not only modify the built-in state, it can add new state variables and behaviors through a registration system.
- It is difficult to precisely control stream output, due to the above issues, the way code and data are mixed in streaming code, and the use of operator overloading (which may select a different overload than you expect).
- The practice of building up output through chains of `<<` operators interferes with internationalization, because it bakes word order into the code, and streams' support for localization is flawed.
- The streams API is subtle and complex, so programmers must develop experience with it in order to use it effectively.
- Resolving the many overloads of `<<` is extremely costly for the compiler. When used pervasively in a large code base, it can consume as much as 20% of the parsing and semantic analysis time.

Use streams only when they are the best tool for the job. This is typically the case when the I/O is ad-hoc, local, human-readable, and targeted at other developers rather than end-users. Be consistent with the code around you, and with the codebase as a whole; if there's an established tool for your problem, use that tool instead. In particular, logging libraries are usually a better choice than std::cerr or std::clog for diagnostic output, and the libraries in absl/strings or the equivalent are usually a better choice than std::stringstream.

Avoid using streams for I/O that faces external users or handles untrusted data. Instead, find and use the appropriate templating libraries to handle issues like internationalization, localization, and security hardening.

If you do use streams, avoid the stateful parts of the streams API (other than error state), such as imbue(), xalloc(), and register_callback(). Use explicit formatting functions (see e.g. absl/strings) rather than stream manipulators or formatting flags to control formatting details such as number base, precision, or padding.

Overload << as a streaming operator for your type only if your type represents a value, and << writes out a human-readable string representation of that value. Avoid exposing implementation details in the output of <<; if you need to print object internals for debugging, use named functions instead (a method named DebugString() is the most common convention).

Preincrement and Predecrement

Use prefix form (++i) of the increment and decrement operators with iterators and other template objects.

When a variable is incremented (++i or i++) or decremented (--i or i--) and the value of the expression is not used, one must decide whether to preincrement (decrement) or postincrement (decrement).

When the return value is ignored, the "pre" form (++i) is never less efficient than the "post" form (i++), and is often more efficient. This is because post-increment (or decrement) requires a copy of i to be made, which is the value of the expression. If i is an iterator or other non-scalar type, copying i could be expensive. Since the two types of increment behave the same when the value is ignored, why not just always pre-increment?

The tradition developed, in C, of using post-increment when the expression value is not used, especially in for loops. Some find post-increment easier to read, since the "subject" (i) precedes the "verb" (++), just like in English.

For simple scalar (non-object) values there is no reason to prefer one form and we allow either. For iterators and other template types, use pre-increment.

Use of const

In APIs, use const whenever it makes sense. constexpr is a better choice for some uses of const.

Declared variables and parameters can be preceded by the keyword const to indicate the variables are not changed (e.g., const int foo). Class functions can have the const qualifier to indicate the function does not change the state of the class member variables (e.g., class Foo { int Bar(char c) const; };).

Easier for people to understand how variables are being used. Allows the compiler to do better type checking, and, conceivably, generate better code. Helps people convince themselves of program correctness because they know the functions they call are limited in how they can modify your variables. Helps people know what functions are safe to use without locks in multi-threaded programs.

const is viral: if you pass a const variable to a function, that function must have const in its prototype (or the variable will need a const_cast). This can be a particular problem when calling library functions.

We strongly recommend using const in APIs (i.e. on function parameters, methods, and non-local variables) wherever it is meaningful and accurate. This provides consistent, mostly compiler-verified documentation of what objects an operation can mutate. Having a consistent and reliable way to distinguish reads from writes is critical to writing thread-safe code, and is useful in many other contexts as well. In particular:

- If a function guarantees that it will not modify an argument passed by reference or by pointer, the corresponding function parameter should be a reference-to-const (const T&) or pointer-to-const (const T*), respectively.
- For a function parameter passed by value, const has no effect on the caller, thus is not recommended in function declarations. See TotW #109.
- Declare methods to be const unless they alter the logical state of the object (or enable the user to modify that state, e.g. by returning a non-const reference, but that's rare), or they can't safely be invoked concurrently.

Using const on local variables is neither encouraged nor discouraged.

All of a class's const operations should be safe to invoke concurrently with each other. If that's not feasible, the class must be clearly documented as "thread-unsafe".

Where to put the const

Some people favor the form int const *foo to const int* foo . They argue that this is more readable because it's more consistent: it keeps the rule that const always follows the object it's describing. However, this consistency argument doesn't apply in codebases with few deeply-nested pointer expressions since
most const expressions have only one const , and it applies to the

underlying value. In such cases, there's no consistency to maintain. Putting the const first is arguably more readable, since it follows English in putting the "adjective" (const) before the "noun" (int).

That said, while we encourage putting const first, we do not require it. But be consistent with the code around you!

Use of constexpr

Use constexpr to define true constants or to ensure constant initialization.

Some variables can be declared constexpr to indicate the variables are true constants, i.e. fixed at compilation/link time. Some functions and constructors can be declared constexpr which enables them to be used in defining a constexpr variable.

Use of constexpr enables definition of constants with floating-point expressions rather than just literals; definition of constants of user-defined types; and definition of constants with function calls.

Prematurely marking something as constexpr may cause migration problems if later on it has to be downgraded. Current restrictions on what is allowed in constexpr functions and constructors may invite obscure workarounds in these definitions.

constexpr definitions enable a more robust specification of the constant parts of an interface. Use constexpr to specify true constants and the functions that support their definitions. Avoid complexifying function definitions to enable their use with constexpr . Do not use constexpr to force inlining.

Integer Types

Of the built-in C++ integer types, the only one used is int . If a program needs a variable of a different size, use a precise-width integer type from <stdint.h> , such as int16_t . If your variable represents a value that could ever be greater than or equal to 2^{31} (2GiB), use a 64-bit type such as int64_t . Keep in mind that even if your value won't ever be too large for an `int`, it may be used in intermediate calculations which may require a larger type. When in doubt, choose a larger type.

C++ does not specify the sizes of integer types like `int`. Typically people assume that `short` is 16 bits, `int` is 32 bits, `long` is 32 bits and `long long` is 64 bits.

Uniformity of declaration.

The sizes of integral types in C++ can vary based on compiler and architecture.

`<cstdint>` defines types like `int16_t`, `uint32_t`, `int64_t`, etc. You should always use those in preference to `short`, `unsigned long long` and the like, when you need a guarantee on the size of an integer. Of the C integer types, only `int` should be used. When appropriate, you are welcome to use standard types like `size_t` and `ptrdiff_t`.

We use `int` very often, for integers we know are not going to be too big, e.g., loop counters. Use plain old `int` for such things. You should assume that an `int` is at least 32 bits, but don't assume that it has more than 32 bits. If you need a 64-bit integer type, use `int64_t` or `uint64_t`.

For integers we know can be "big", use `int64_t`.

You should not use the unsigned integer types such as `uint32_t`, unless there is a valid reason such as representing a bit pattern rather than a number, or you need defined overflow modulo 2^N. In particular, do not use unsigned types to say a number will never be negative. Instead, use assertions for this.

If your code is a container that returns a size, be sure to use a type that will accommodate any possible usage of your container. When in doubt, use a larger type rather than a smaller type.

Use care when converting integer types. Integer conversions and promotions can cause undefined behavior, leading to security bugs and other problems.

On Unsigned Integers

Unsigned integers are good for representing bitfields and modular arithmetic. Because of historical accident, the C++ standard also uses unsigned integers to represent the size of containers - many members of the standards body believe this to be a mistake, but it is effectively impossible to fix at this point. The fact that unsigned arithmetic doesn't model the behavior of a simple integer, but is instead defined by the standard to model modular arithmetic (wrapping around on overflow/underflow), means that a significant class of bugs cannot be diagnosed by the compiler. In other cases, the defined behavior impedes optimization.

That said, mixing signedness of integer types is responsible for an equally large class of problems. The best advice we can provide: try to use iterators and containers rather than pointers and sizes, try not to mix signedness, and try to avoid unsigned types (except for representing bitfields or modular arithmetic). Do not use an unsigned type merely to assert that a variable is non-negative.

64-bit Portability

Code should be 64-bit and 32-bit friendly. Bear in mind problems of printing, comparisons, and structure alignment.

- Correct portable printf() conversion specifiers for some integral typedefs rely on macro expansions that we find unpleasant to use and impractical to require (the PRI macros from <cinttypes>). Unless there is no reasonable alternative for your particular case, try to avoid or even upgrade APIs that rely on the printf family. Instead use a library supporting typesafe numeric formatting, such as StrCat or Substitute for fast simple conversions, or std::ostream .

Unfortunately, the PRI macros are the only portable way to specify a conversion for the standard bitwidth typedefs (e.g. int64_t, uint64_t, int32_t, uint32_t, etc). Where possible, avoid passing arguments of types specified by bitwidth typedefs to printf-based APIs. Note that it is acceptable to use typedefs for which printf has dedicated length modifiers, such as size_t (z), ptrdiff_t (t), and maxint_t (j).

- Remember that sizeof(void *) != sizeof(int). Use intptr_t if you want a pointer-sized integer.
- You may need to be careful with structure alignments, particularly for structures being stored on disk. Any class/structure with a int64_t / uint64_t member will by default end up being 8-byte aligned on a 64-bit system. If you have such structures being shared on disk between 32-bit and 64-bit code, you will need to ensure that they are packed the same on both architectures. Most compilers offer a way to alter structure alignment. For gcc, you can use __attribute__((packed)). MSVC offers #pragma pack() and __declspec(align()).
- Use braced-initialization as needed to create 64-bit constants. For example:

> - int64_t my_value{0x123456789};
> - uint64_t my_mask{3ULL << 48};

Preprocessor Macros

Avoid defining macros, especially in headers; prefer inline functions, enums, and const variables. Name macros with a project-specific prefix. Do not use macros to define pieces of a C++ API.

Macros mean that the code you see is not the same as the code the compiler sees. This can introduce unexpected behavior, especially since macros have global scope.

The problems introduced by macros are especially severe when they are used to define pieces of a C++ API, and still more so for public APIs. Every error message from the compiler when developers incorrectly use that interface now must explain how the macros formed the interface. Refactoring and analysis tools have a dramatically harder time updating the interface. As a consequence, we specifically disallow using macros in this way. For example, avoid patterns like:

```
class WOMBAT_TYPE(Foo) {
  // ...

public:
  EXPAND_PUBLIC_WOMBAT_API(Foo)

  EXPAND_WOMBAT_COMPARISONS(Foo, ==, <)
};
```

Luckily, macros are not nearly as necessary in C++ as they are in C. Instead of using a macro to inline performance-critical code, use an inline function. Instead of using a macro to store a constant, use a const variable. Instead of using a macro to "abbreviate" a long variable name, use a reference. Instead of using a macro to conditionally compile code ... well, don't do that at all (except, of course, for the #define guards to prevent double inclusion of header files). It makes testing much more difficult.

Macros can do things these other techniques cannot, and you do see them in the codebase, especially in the lower-level libraries. And some of their special features (like stringifying, concatenation, and so forth) are not available through the language proper. But before using a macro, consider carefully whether there's a non-macro way to achieve the same result. If you need to use a macro to define an interface, contact your project leads to request a waiver of this rule.

The following usage pattern will avoid many problems with macros; if you use macros, follow it whenever possible:

- Don't define macros in a .h file.
- #define macros right before you use them, and #undef them right after.
- Do not just #undef an existing macro before replacing it with your own; instead, pick a name that's likely to be unique.
- Try not to use macros that expand to unbalanced C++ constructs, or at least document that behavior well.
- Prefer not using ## to generate function/class/variable names.

Exporting macros from headers (i.e. defining them in a header without #undefing them before the end of the header) is extremely strongly discouraged. If you do export a macro from a header, it must have a globally unique name. To achieve this, it must be named with a prefix consisting of your project's namespace name (but upper case).

0 and nullptr/NULL

Use nullptr for pointers, and '\0' for chars (and not the 0 literal).

For pointers (address values), use nullptr, as this provides type-safety.

For C++03 projects, prefer NULL to 0. While the values are equivalent, NULL looks more like a pointer to the reader, and some C++ compilers provide special definitions of NULL which enable them to give useful warnings. Never use NULL for numeric (integer or floating-point) values.

Use '\0' for the null character. Using the correct type makes the code more readable.

sizeof

Prefer sizeof(*varname*) to sizeof(*type*).

Use sizeof(*varname*) when you take the size of a particular variable. sizeof(*varname*) will update appropriately if someone changes the variable type either now or later. You may use sizeof(*type*) for code unrelated to any particular variable, such as code that manages an external or internal data format where a variable of an appropriate C++ type is not convenient.

```
struct data;
memset(&data, 0, sizeof(data));
```

```
memset(&data, 0, sizeof(Struct));
```

```
if (raw_size < sizeof(int)) {
  LOG(ERROR) << "compressed record not big enough for count: " << raw_size;
  return false;
}
```

Type deduction

Use type deduction only if it makes the code clearer to readers who aren't familiar with the project, or if it makes the code safer. Do not use it merely to avoid the inconvenience of writing an explicit type.

There are several contexts in which C++ allows (or even requires) types to be deduced by the compiler, rather than spelled out explicitly in the code:

Function template argument deduction

A function template can be invoked without explicit template arguments. The compiler deduces those arguments from the types of the function arguments:

```
template <typename T>
void f(T t);

f(0);  // Invokes f<int>(0)
```

auto variable declarations

A variable declaration can use the auto keyword in place of the type. The compiler deduces the type from the variable's initializer, following the same rules as function template argument deduction with the same initializer (so long as you don't use curly braces instead of parentheses).

```
auto a = 42;  // a is an int
auto& b = a;  // b is an int&
auto c = b;   // c is an int
auto d{42};   // d is an int, not a std::initializer_list<int>
```

auto can be qualified with const, and can be used as part of a pointer or reference type, but it can't be used as a template argument. A rare variant of this syntax uses decltype(auto) instead of auto, in which case the deduced type is the result of applying decltype to the initializer.

Function return type deduction

auto (and decltype(auto)) can also be used in place of a function return type. The compiler deduces the return type from the return statements in the function body, following the same rules as for variable declarations:

```
auto f() { return 0; }  // The return type of f is int
```

Lambda expression return types can be deduced in the same way, but this is triggered by omitting the return type, rather than by an explicit auto. Confusingly, trailing return type syntax for functions also uses auto in the return-type position, but that doesn't rely on type deduction; it's just an alternate syntax for an explicit return type.

Generic lambdas

A lambda expression can use the auto keyword in place of one or more of its parameter types. This causes the lambda's call operator to be a function template instead of an ordinary function, with a separate template parameter for each auto function parameter:

```
// Sort `vec` in increasing order
std::sort(vec.begin(), vec.end(), [](auto lhs, auto rhs) { return lhs > rhs; });
```

Lambda init captures

Lambda captures can have explicit initializers, which can be used to declare wholly new variables rather than only capturing existing ones:

```
[x = 42, y = "foo"] { ... }  // x is an int, and y is a const char*
```

This syntax doesn't allow the type to be specified; instead, it's deduced using the rules for auto variables.

Class template argument deduction

See below.

Structured bindings

When declaring a tuple, struct, or array using auto, you can specify names for the individual elements instead of a name for the whole object; these names are called "structured bindings", and the whole declaration is called a "structured binding declaration". This syntax provides no way of specifying the type of either the enclosing object or the individual names:

```
auto [iter, success] = my_map.insert({key, value});
if (!success) {
```

```
    iter->second = value;
}
```

The auto can also be qualified with const, &, and &&, but note that these qualifiers technically apply to the anonymous tuple/struct/array, rather than the individual bindings. The rules that determine the types of the bindings are quite complex; the results tend to be unsurprising, except that the binding types typically won't be references even if the declaration declares a reference (but they will usually behave like references anyway).

(These summaries omit many details and caveats; see the links for further information.)

- C++ type names can be long and cumbersome, especially when they involve templates or namespaces.
- When a C++ type name is repeated within a single declaration or a small code region, the repetition may not be aiding readability.
- It is sometimes safer to let the type be deduced, since that avoids the possibility of unintended copies or type conversions.

C++ code is usually clearer when types are explicit, especially when type deduction would depend on information from distant parts of the code. In expressions like:

```
auto foo = x.add_foo();
auto i = y.Find(key);
```

it may not be obvious what the resulting types are if the type of y isn't very well known, or if y was declared many lines earlier.

Programmers have to understand when type deduction will or won't produce a reference type, or they'll get copies when they didn't mean to.

If a deduced type is used as part of an interface, then a programmer might change its type while only intending to change its value, leading to a more radical API change than intended.

The fundamental rule is: use type deduction only to make the code clearer or safer, and do not use it merely to avoid the inconvenience of writing an explicit type. When judging whether the code is clearer, keep in mind that your readers are not necessarily on your team, or familiar with your project, so types that you and your reviewer experience as as unnecessary clutter will very often provide useful information to others. For example, you can assume that the return type of make_unique<Foo>() is obvious, but the return type of MyWidgetFactory() probably isn't.

These principles applies to all forms of type deduction, but the details vary, as described in the following sections.

Function template argument deduction

Function template argument deduction is almost always OK. Type deduction is the expected default way of interacting with function templates, because it allows function templates to act like infinite sets of ordinary function overloads. Consequently, function templates are almost always designed so that template argument deduction is clear and safe, or doesn't compile.

Local variable type deduction

For local variables, you can use type deduction to make the code clearer by eliminating type information that is obvious or irrelevant, so that the reader can focus on the meaningful parts of the code:

```
std::unique_ptr<WidgetWithBellsAndWhistles> widget_ptr =
    absl::make_unique<WidgetWithBellsAndWhistles>(arg1, arg2);
absl::flat_hash_map<std::string,
```

```
            std::unique_ptr<WidgetWithBellsAndWhistles>>::con
st_iterator
    it = my_map_.find(key);
std::array<int, 0> numbers = {4, 8, 15, 16, 23, 42};
auto widget_ptr =
absl::make_unique<WidgetWithBellsAndWhistles>(arg1, arg2);
auto it = my_map_.find(key);
std::array numbers = {4, 8, 15, 16, 23, 42};
```

Types sometimes contain a mixture of useful information and boilerplate, such as it in the example above: it's obvious that the type is an iterator, and in many contexts the container type and even the key type aren't relevant, but the type of the values is probably useful. In such situations, it's often possible to define local variables with explicit types that convey the relevant information:

```
auto it = my_map_.find(key);
if (it != my_map_.end()) {
  WidgetWithBellsAndWhistles& widget = *it->second;
  // Do stuff with `widget`
}
```

If the type is a template instance, and the parameters are boilerplate but the template itself is informative, you can use class template argument deduction to suppress the boilerplate. However, cases where this actually provides a meaningful benefit are quite rare. Note that class template argument deduction is also subject to a separate style rule.

Do not use decltype(auto) if a simpler option will work, because it's a fairly obscure feature, so it has a high cost in code clarity.

Return type deduction

Use return type deduction (for both functions and lambdas) only if the function body has a very small number of return statements, and very little other code, because otherwise the reader may not be able to tell at a glance what the return type is. Furthermore, use it only if the function or lambda has a very narrow scope, because functions with deduced return types don't define abstraction boundaries: the implementation *is* the interface. In particular, public functions in header files should almost never have deduced return types.

Parameter type deduction

auto parameter types for lambdas should be used with caution, because the actual type is determined by the code that calls the lambda, rather than by the definition of the lambda. Consequently, an explicit type will almost always be clearer unless the lambda is explicitly called very close to where it's defined (so that the reader can easily see both), or the lambda is passed to an interface so well-known that it's obvious what arguments it will eventually be called with (e.g. the std::sort example above).

Lambda init captures

Init captures are covered by a more specific style rule, which largely supersedes the general rules for type deduction.

Structured bindings

Unlike other forms of type deduction, structured bindings can actually give the reader additional information, by giving meaningful names to the elements of a larger object. This means that a structured binding declaration may provide a net readability improvement over an explicit type, even in cases where auto would not. Structured bindings are especially beneficial when the object is a pair or tuple (as in the insert example above), because they don't have meaningful field names to begin with, but note that you generally shouldn't use pairs or tuples unless a pre-existing API like insert forces you to.

If the object being bound is a struct, it may sometimes be helpful to provide names that are more specific to your usage, but keep in mind that this may also mean the names are less recognizable to your reader than the field names. We recommend using a comment to indicate the name of the underlying field, if it doesn't match the name of the binding, using the same syntax as for function parameter comments:

```
auto [/*field_name1=*/ bound_name1, /*field_name2=*/ bound_name2] = ...
```

As with function parameter comments, this can enable tools to detect if you get the order of the fields wrong.

Class template argument deduction

Use class template argument deduction only with templates that have explicitly opted into supporting it.

Class template argument deduction (often abbreviated "CTAD") occurs when a variable is declared with a type that names a template, and the template argument list is not provided (not even empty angle brackets):

```
std::array a = {1, 2, 3};  // `a` is a std::array<int, 3>
```

The compiler deduces the arguments from the initializer using the template's "deduction guides", which can be explicit or implicit.

Explicit deduction guides look like function declarations with trailing return types, except that there's no leading auto , and the function name is the name of the template. For example, the above example relies on this deduction guide for std::array :

```
namespace std {
template <class T, class... U>
```

```
    array(T, U...) -> std::array<T, 1 + sizeof...(U)>;
}
```

Constructors in a primary template (as opposed to a template specialization) also implicitly define deduction guides.

When you declare a variable that relies on CTAD, the compiler selects a deduction guide using the rules of constructor overload resolution, and that guide's return type becomes the type of the variable.

CTAD can sometimes allow you to omit boilerplate from your code.

The implicit deduction guides that are generated from constructors may have undesirable behavior, or be outright incorrect. This is particularly problematic for constructors written before CTAD was introduced in C++17, because the authors of those constructors had no way of knowing about (much less fixing) any problems that their constructors would cause for CTAD. Furthermore, adding explicit deduction guides to fix those problems might break any existing code that relies on the implicit deduction guides.

CTAD also suffers from many of the same drawbacks as auto, because they are both mechanisms for deducing all or part of a variable's type from its initializer. CTAD does give the reader more information than auto, but it also doesn't give the reader an obvious cue that information has been omitted.

Do not use CTAD with a given template unless the template's maintainers have opted into supporting use of CTAD by providing at least one explicit deduction guide (all templates in the std namespace are also presumed to have opted in). This should be enforced with a compiler warning if available.

Uses of CTAD must also follow the general rules on Type deduction.

Lambda expressions

Use lambda expressions where appropriate. Prefer explicit captures when the lambda will escape the current scope.

Lambda expressions are a concise way of creating anonymous function objects. They're often useful when passing functions as arguments. For example:

```
std::sort(v.begin(), v.end(), [](int x, int y) {
  return Weight(x) < Weight(y);
});
```

They further allow capturing variables from the enclosing scope either explicitly by name, or implicitly using a default capture. Explicit captures require each variable to be listed, as either a value or reference capture:

```
int weight = 3;
int sum = 0;
// Captures `weight` by value and `sum` by reference.
std::for_each(v.begin(), v.end(), [weight, &sum](int x) {
  sum += weight * x;
});
```

Default captures implicitly capture any variable referenced in the lambda body, including this if any members are used:

```
const std::vector<int> lookup_table = ...;
std::vector<int> indices = ...;
// Captures `lookup_table` by reference, sorts `indices` by the value
// of the associated element in `lookup_table`.
std::sort(indices.begin(), indices.end(), [&](int a, int b) {
  return lookup_table[a] < lookup_table[b];
});
```

A variable capture can also have an explicit initializer, which can be used for capturing move-only variables by value, or for other situations not handled by ordinary reference or value captures:

```
std::unique_ptr<Foo> foo = ...;
[foo = std::move(foo)] () {
  ...
}
```

Such captures (often called "init captures" or "generalized lambda captures") need not actually "capture" anything from the enclosing scope, or even have a name from the enclosing scope; this syntax is a fully general way to define members of a lambda object:

```
[foo = std::vector<int>({1, 2, 3})] () {
  ...
}
```

The type of a capture with an initializer is deduced using the same rules as auto.

- Lambdas are much more concise than other ways of defining function objects to be passed to STL algorithms, which can be a readability improvement.
- Appropriate use of default captures can remove redundancy and highlight important exceptions from the default.
- Lambdas, std::function, and std::bind can be used in combination as a general purpose callback mechanism; they make it easy to write functions that take bound functions as arguments.

- Variable capture in lambdas can be a source of dangling-pointer bugs, particularly if a lambda escapes the current scope.
- Default captures by value can be misleading because they do not prevent dangling-pointer bugs. Capturing a pointer by value doesn't cause a deep copy, so it often has the

same lifetime issues as capture by reference. This is especially confusing when capturing 'this' by value, since the use of 'this' is often implicit.
- Captures actually declare new variables (whether or not the captures have initializers), but they look nothing like any other variable declaration syntax in C++. In particular, there's no place for the variable's type, or even an auto placeholder (although init captures can indicate it indirectly, e.g. with a cast). This can make it difficult to even recognize them as declarations.
- Init captures inherently rely on type deduction, and suffer from many of the same drawbacks as auto, with the additional problem that the syntax doesn't even cue the reader that deduction is taking place.
- It's possible for use of lambdas to get out of hand; very long nested anonymous functions can make code harder to understand.

- Use lambda expressions where appropriate, with formatting as described below.
- Prefer explicit captures if the lambda may escape the current scope. For example, instead of:

- {
-   Foo foo;
- ...
-   executor->Schedule([&] { Frobnicate(foo); })
- ...
- }
- // BAD! The fact that the lambda makes use of a reference to `foo` and

- // possibly `this` (if `Frobnicate` is a member function) may not be
- // apparent on a cursory inspection. If the lambda is invoked after
- // the function returns, that would be bad, because both `foo`
- // and the enclosing object could have been destroyed.

prefer to write:

```
{
  Foo foo;
  ...
  executor->Schedule([&foo] { Frobnicate(foo); })
  ...
}
// BETTER - The compile will fail if `Frobnicate` is a member
// function, and it's clearer that `foo` is dangerously captured by
// reference.
```

- Use default capture by reference ([&]) only when the lifetime of the lambda is obviously shorter than any potential captures.
- Use default capture by value ([=]) only as a means of binding a few variables for a short lambda, where the set of captured variables is obvious at a glance. Prefer not to write long or complex lambdas with default capture by value.
- Use captures only to actually capture variables from the enclosing scope. Do not use captures with initializers to introduce new names, or to substantially change the meaning of an existing name. Instead, declare a new variable in the conventional way and then capture it, or

avoid the lambda shorthand and define a function object explicitly.
- See the section on <u>type deduction</u> for guidance on specifying the parameter and return types.

Template metaprogramming

Avoid complicated template programming.

Template metaprogramming refers to a family of techniques that exploit the fact that the C++ template instantiation mechanism is Turing complete and can be used to perform arbitrary compile-time computation in the type domain.

Template metaprogramming allows extremely flexible interfaces that are type safe and high performance. Facilities like std::tuple , std::function , and Boost.Spirit would be impossible without it.

The techniques used in template metaprogramming are often obscure to anyone but language experts. Code that uses templates in complicated ways is often unreadable and is hard to debug or maintain.

Template metaprogramming often leads to extremely poor compile time error messages: even if an interface is simple, the complicated implementation details become visible when the user does something wrong.

Template metaprogramming interferes with large scale refactoring by making the job of refactoring tools harder. First, the template code is expanded in multiple contexts, and it's hard to verify that the transformation makes sense in all of them. Second, some refactoring tools work with an AST that only represents the structure of the code after template expansion. It can be difficult to automatically work back to the original source construct that needs to be rewritten.

Template metaprogramming sometimes allows cleaner and easier-to-use interfaces than would be possible without it, but it's also often a temptation to be overly clever. It's best used in a small number of low level components where the extra maintenance burden is spread out over a large number of uses.

Think twice before using template metaprogramming or other complicated template techniques; think about whether the average member of your team will be able to understand your code well enough to maintain it after you switch to another project, or whether a non-C++ programmer or someone casually browsing the code base will be able to understand the error messages or trace the flow of a function they want to call. If you're using recursive template instantiations or type lists or metafunctions or expression templates, or relying on SFINAE or on the sizeof trick for detecting function overload resolution, then there's a good chance you've gone too far.

If you use template metaprogramming, you should expect to put considerable effort into minimizing and isolating the complexity. You should hide metaprogramming as an implementation detail whenever possible, so that user-facing headers are readable, and you should make sure that tricky code is especially well commented. You should carefully document how the code is used, and you should say something about what the "generated" code looks like. Pay extra attention to the error messages that the compiler emits when users make mistakes. The error messages are part of your user interface, and your code should be tweaked as necessary so that the error messages are understandable and actionable from a user point of view.

Boost

Use only approved libraries from the Boost library collection.

The Boost library collection is a popular collection of peer-reviewed, free, open-source C++ libraries.

Boost code is generally very high-quality, is widely portable, and fills many important gaps in the C++ standard library, such as type traits and better binders.

Some Boost libraries encourage coding practices which can hamper readability, such as metaprogramming and other advanced template techniques, and an excessively "functional" style of programming.

In order to maintain a high level of readability for all contributors who might read and maintain code, we only allow an approved subset of Boost features. Currently, the following libraries are permitted:

- Call Traits from boost/call_traits.hpp
- Compressed Pair from boost/compressed_pair.hpp
- The Boost Graph Library (BGL) from boost/graph, except serialization (adj_list_serialize.hpp) and parallel/distributed algorithms and data structures (boost/graph/parallel/* and boost/graph/distributed/*).
- Property Map from boost/property_map, except parallel/distributed property maps (boost/property_map/parallel/*).
- Iterator from boost/iterator
- The part of Polygon that deals with Voronoi diagram construction and doesn't depend on the rest of Polygon: boost/polygon/voronoi_builder.hpp , boost/polygon/voronoi_diagram.hpp , and boost/polygon/voronoi_geometry_type.hpp
- Bimap from boost/bimap
- Statistical Distributions and Functions from boost/math/distributions
- Special Functions from boost/math/special_functions
- Root Finding Functions from boost/math/tools
- Multi-index from boost/multi_index
- Heap from boost/heap

- The flat containers from <u>Container</u>: boost/container/flat_map , and boost/container/flat_set
- <u>Intrusive</u> from boost/intrusive .
- The <u>boost/sort library</u>.
- <u>Preprocessor</u> from boost/preprocessor .

We are actively considering adding other Boost features to the list, so this list may be expanded in the future.

std::hash

Do not define specializations of std::hash .

std::hash<T> is the function object that the C++11 hash containers use to hash keys of type T , unless the user explicitly specifies a different hash function. For example, std::unordered_map<int, std::string> is a hash map that uses std::hash<int> to hash its keys, whereas std::unordered_map<int, std::string, MyIntHash> uses MyIntHash .

std::hash is defined for all integral, floating-point, pointer, and enum types, as well as some standard library types such as string and unique_ptr . Users can enable it to work for their own types by defining specializations of it for those types.

std::hash is easy to use, and simplifies the code since you don't have to name it explicitly. Specializing std::hash is the standard way of specifying how to hash a type, so it's what outside resources will teach, and what new engineers will expect.

std::hash is hard to specialize. It requires a lot of boilerplate code, and more importantly, it combines responsibility for identifying the hash inputs with responsibility for executing the hashing algorithm itself. The type author has to be responsible for the former, but the latter requires expertise that a type author usually doesn't have, and shouldn't need. The stakes here are high because low-quality hash functions can be security vulnerabilities, due to the emergence of [hash flooding attacks](#).

Even for experts, `std::hash` specializations are inordinately difficult to implement correctly for compound types, because the implementation cannot recursively call `std::hash` on data members. High-quality hash algorithms maintain large amounts of internal state, and reducing that state to the `size_t` bytes that `std::hash` returns is usually the slowest part of the computation, so it should not be done more than once.

Due to exactly that issue, `std::hash` does not work with `std::pair` or `std::tuple`, and the language does not allow us to extend it to support them.

You can use `std::hash` with the types that it supports "out of the box", but do not specialize it to support additional types. If you need a hash table with a key type that `std::hash` does not support, consider using legacy hash containers (e.g. `hash_map`) for now; they use a different default hasher, which is unaffected by this prohibition.

If you want to use the standard hash containers anyway, you will need to specify a custom hasher for the key type, e.g.

```
std::unordered_map<MyKeyType, Value, MyKeyTypeHasher> my_map;
```

Consult with the type's owners to see if there is an existing hasher that you can use; otherwise work with them to provide one, or roll your own.

We are planning to provide a hash function that can work with any type, using a new customization mechanism that doesn't have the drawbacks of `std::hash`.

Other C++ Features

As with Boost, some modern C++ extensions encourage coding practices that hamper readability—for example by removing checked redundancy (such as type names) that may be helpful to readers, or by encouraging template metaprogramming. Other extensions duplicate functionality available through existing mechanisms, which may lead to confusion and conversion costs.

In addition to what's described in the rest of the style guide, the following C++ features may not be used:

- Compile-time rational numbers (<ratio>), because of concerns that it's tied to a more template-heavy interface style.
- The <cfenv> and <fenv.h> headers, because many compilers do not support those features reliably.
- The <filesystem> header, which does not have sufficient support for testing, and suffers from inherent security vulnerabilities.

Nonstandard Extensions

Nonstandard extensions to C++ may not be used unless otherwise specified.

Compilers support various extensions that are not part of standard C++. Such extensions include GCC's __attribute__ , intrinsic functions such as __builtin_prefetch , designated initializers (e.g. Foo f = {.field = 3}), inline assembly, __COUNTER__ , __PRETTY_FUNCTION__ , compound statement expressions (e.g. foo = ({ int x; Bar(&x); x }) , variable-length arrays and alloca() , and the "Elvis Operator" a?:b .

- Nonstandard extensions may provide useful features that do not exist in standard C++. For example, some people think that designated initializers are more readable than standard C++ features like constructors.

- Important performance guidance to the compiler can only be specified using extensions.
- Nonstandard extensions do not work in all compilers. Use of nonstandard extensions reduces portability of code.
- Even if they are supported in all targeted compilers, the extensions are often not well-specified, and there may be subtle behavior differences between compilers.
- Nonstandard extensions add to the language features that a reader must know to understand the code.

Do not use nonstandard extensions. You may use portability wrappers that are implemented using nonstandard extensions, so long as those wrappers are provided by a designated project-wide portability header.

Aliases

Public aliases are for the benefit of an API's user, and should be clearly documented.

There are several ways to create names that are aliases of other entities:

```
typedef Foo Bar;
using Bar = Foo;
using other_namespace::Foo;
```

In new code, using is preferable to typedef, because it provides a more consistent syntax with the rest of C++ and works with templates.

Like other declarations, aliases declared in a header file are part of that header's public API unless they're in a function definition, in the private portion of a class, or in an explicitly-marked internal namespace. Aliases in such areas or in .cc files are implementation details (because client code can't refer to them), and are not restricted by this rule.

- Aliases can improve readability by simplifying a long or complicated name.
- Aliases can reduce duplication by naming in one place a type used repeatedly in an API, which *might* make it easier to change the type later.

- When placed in a header where client code can refer to them, aliases increase the number of entities in that header's API, increasing its complexity.
- Clients can easily rely on unintended details of public aliases, making changes difficult.
- It can be tempting to create a public alias that is only intended for use in the implementation, without considering its impact on the API, or on maintainability.
- Aliases can create risk of name collisions
- Aliases can reduce readability by giving a familiar construct an unfamiliar name
- Type aliases can create an unclear API contract: it is unclear whether the alias is guaranteed to be identical to the type it aliases, to have the same API, or only to be usable in specified narrow ways

Don't put an alias in your public API just to save typing in the implementation; do so only if you intend it to be used by your clients.

When defining a public alias, document the intent of the new name, including whether it is guaranteed to always be the same as the type it's currently aliased to, or whether a more limited compatibility is intended. This lets the user know whether they can treat the types as substitutable or whether more specific rules must be followed, and can help the implementation retain some degree of freedom to change the alias.

Don't put namespace aliases in your public API. (See also Namespaces).

For example, these aliases document how they are intended to be used in client code:

```
namespace mynamespace {
// Used to store field measurements. DataPoint may change from Bar* to some internal type.
// Client code should treat it as an opaque pointer.
using DataPoint = foo::Bar*;

// A set of measurements. Just an alias for user convenience.
using TimeSeries = std::unordered_set<DataPoint, std::hash<DataPoint>, DataPointComparator>;
} // namespace mynamespace
```

These aliases don't document intended use, and half of them aren't meant for client use:

```
namespace mynamespace {
// Bad: none of these say how they should be used.
using DataPoint = foo::Bar*;
using std::unordered_set;  // Bad: just for local convenience
using std::hash;           // Bad: just for local convenience
typedef unordered_set<DataPoint, hash<DataPoint>, DataPointComparator> TimeSeries;
} // namespace mynamespace
```

However, local convenience aliases are fine in function definitions, private sections of classes, explicitly marked internal namespaces, and in .cc files:

```
// In a .cc file
```

```
using foo::Bar;
```

Naming

The most important consistency rules are those that govern naming. The style of a name immediately informs us what sort of thing the named entity is: a type, a variable, a function, a constant, a macro, etc., without requiring us to search for the declaration of that entity. The pattern-matching engine in our brains relies a great deal on these naming rules.

Naming rules are pretty arbitrary, but we feel that consistency is more important than individual preferences in this area, so regardless of whether you find them sensible or not, the rules are the rules.

General Naming Rules

Optimize for readability using names that would be clear even to people on a different team.

Use names that describe the purpose or intent of the object. Do not worry about saving horizontal space as it is far more important to make your code immediately understandable by a new reader. Minimize the use of abbreviations that would likely be unknown to someone outside your project (especially acronyms and initialisms). Do not abbreviate by deleting letters within a word. As a rule of thumb, an abbreviation is probably OK if it's listed in Wikipedia. Generally speaking, descriptiveness should be proportional to the name's scope of visibility. For example, n may be a fine name within a 5-line function, but within the scope of a class, it's likely too vague.

```
class MyClass {
public:
  int CountFooErrors(const std::vector<Foo>& foos) {
```

```cpp
    int n = 0;  // Clear meaning given limited scope and context
    for (const auto& foo : foos) {
      ...
      ++n;
    }
    return n;
  }
  void DoSomethingImportant() {
    std::string fqdn = ...;  // Well-known abbreviation for Fully Qualified Domain Name
  }
 private:
  const int kMaxAllowedConnections = ...;  // Clear meaning within context
};
```

```cpp
class MyClass {
 public:
  int CountFooErrors(const std::vector<Foo>& foos) {
    int total_number_of_foo_errors = 0;  // Overly verbose given limited scope and context
    for (int foo_index = 0; foo_index < foos.size(); ++foo_index) {  // Use idiomatic `i`
      ...
      ++total_number_of_foo_errors;
    }
    return total_number_of_foo_errors;
  }
  void DoSomethingImportant() {
    int cstmr_id = ...;  // Deletes internal letters
  }
 private:
  const int kNum = ...;  // Unclear meaning within broad scope
};
```

Note that certain universally-known abbreviations are OK, such as i for an iteration variable and T for a template parameter.

For the purposes of the naming rules below, a "word" is anything that you would write in English without internal spaces. This includes abbreviations and acronyms; e.g., for "camel case" or "Pascal case," in which the first letter of each word is capitalized, use a name like StartRpc() , not StartRPC() .

Template parameters should follow the naming style for their category: type template parameters should follow the rules for type names, and non-type template parameters should follow the rules for variable names.

File Names

Filenames should be all lowercase and can include underscores (_) or dashes (-). Follow the convention that your project uses. If there is no consistent local pattern to follow, prefer "_".

Examples of acceptable file names:
- my_useful_class.cc
- my-useful-class.cc
- myusefulclass.cc
- myusefulclass_test.cc // _unittest and _regtest are deprecated.

C++ files should end in .cc and header files should end in .h . Files that rely on being textually included at specific points should end in .inc (see also the section on self-contained headers).

Do not use filenames that already exist in /usr/include , such as db.h .

In general, make your filenames very specific. For example, use http_server_logs.h rather than logs.h . A very common case is to have a pair of files called, e.g., foo_bar.h and foo_bar.cc, defining a class called FooBar.

Type Names

Type names start with a capital letter and have a capital letter for each new word, with no
underscores: MyExcitingClass, MyExcitingEnum.

The names of all types — classes, structs, type aliases, enums, and type template parameters — have the same naming convention. Type names should start with a capital letter and have a capital letter for each new word. No underscores. For example:

```
// classes and structs
class UrlTable { ...
class UrlTableTester { ...
struct UrlTableProperties { ...

// typedefs
typedef hash_map<UrlTableProperties *, std::string> PropertiesMap;

// using aliases
using PropertiesMap = hash_map<UrlTableProperties *, std::string>;

// enums
enum UrlTableErrors { ...
```

Variable Names

The names of variables (including function parameters) and data members are all lowercase, with underscores between words. Data members of classes (but not structs) additionally have trailing

underscores. For
instance: a_local_variable , a_struct_data_member , a_class_data _member_ .

Common Variable names

For example:

```
std::string table_name;  // OK - lowercase with underscore.
```

```
std::string tableName;   // Bad - mixed case.
```

Class Data Members

Data members of classes, both static and non-static, are named like ordinary nonmember variables, but with a trailing underscore.

```
class TableInfo {
  ...
private:
  std::string table_name_;  // OK - underscore at end.
  static Pool<TableInfo>* pool_;  // OK.
};
```

Struct Data Members

Data members of structs, both static and non-static, are named like ordinary nonmember variables. They do not have the trailing underscores that data members in classes have.

```
struct UrlTableProperties {
  std::string name;
  int num_entries;
  static Pool<UrlTableProperties>* pool;
};
```

See Structs vs. Classes for a discussion of when to use a struct versus a class.

Constant Names

Variables declared constexpr or const, and whose value is fixed for the duration of the program, are named with a leading "k" followed by mixed case. Underscores can be used as separators in the rare cases where capitalization cannot be used for separation. For example:

```
const int kDaysInAWeek = 7;
const int kAndroid8_0_0 = 24;  // Android 8.0.0
```

All such variables with static storage duration (i.e. statics and globals, see Storage Duration for details) should be named this way. This convention is optional for variables of other storage classes, e.g. automatic variables, otherwise the usual variable naming rules apply.

Function Names

Regular functions have mixed case; accessors and mutators may be named like variables.

Ordinarily, functions should start with a capital letter and have a capital letter for each new word.

```
AddTableEntry()
DeleteUrl()
OpenFileOrDie()
```

(The same naming rule applies to class- and namespace-scope constants that are exposed as part of an API and that are intended to look like functions, because the fact that they're objects rather than functions is an unimportant implementation detail.)

Accessors and mutators (get and set functions) may be named like variables. These often correspond to actual member variables, but this is not required. For example, int count() and void set_count(int count) .

Namespace Names

Namespace names are all lower-case. Top-level namespace names are based on the project name . Avoid collisions between nested namespaces and well-known top-level namespaces.

The name of a top-level namespace should usually be the name of the project or team whose code is contained in that namespace. The code in that namespace should usually be in a directory whose basename matches the namespace name (or in subdirectories thereof).

Keep in mind that the rule against abbreviated names applies to namespaces just as much as variable names. Code inside the namespace seldom needs to mention the namespace name, so there's usually no particular need for abbreviation anyway.

Avoid nested namespaces that match well-known top-level namespaces. Collisions between namespace names can lead to surprising build breaks because of name lookup rules. In particular, do not create any nested std namespaces. Prefer unique project identifiers (websearch::index , websearch::index_util) over collision-prone names like websearch::util .

For internal namespaces, be wary of other code being added to the same internal namespace causing a collision (internal helpers within a team tend to be related and may lead to collisions). In such a situation, using the filename to make a unique internal name is helpful (websearch::index::frobber_internal for use in frobber.h)

Enumerator Names

Enumerators (for both scoped and unscoped enums) should be named *either* like constants or like macros: either kEnumName or ENUM_NAME.

Preferably, the individual enumerators should be named like constants. However, it is also acceptable to name them like macros. The enumeration name, UrlTableErrors (and AlternateUrlTableErrors), is a type, and therefore mixed case.

```
enum UrlTableErrors {
  kOk = 0,
  kErrorOutOfMemory,
  kErrorMalformedInput,
};
enum AlternateUrlTableErrors {
  OK = 0,
  OUT_OF_MEMORY = 1,
  MALFORMED_INPUT = 2,
};
```

Until January 2009, the style was to name enum values like macros. This caused problems with name collisions between enum values and macros. Hence, the change to prefer constant-style naming was put in place. New code should prefer constant-style naming if possible. However, there is no reason to change old code to use constant-style names, unless the old names are actually causing a compile-time problem.

Macro Names

You're not really going to define a macro, are you? If you do, they're like this: MY_MACRO_THAT_SCARES_SMALL_CHILDREN_AND_ADULTS_ALIKE.

Please see the <u>description of macros</u>; in general macros should *not* be used. However, if they are absolutely needed, then they should be named with all capitals and underscores.

```
#define ROUND(x) ...
#define PI_ROUNDED 3.0
```

Exceptions to Naming Rules

If you are naming something that is analogous to an existing C or C++ entity then you can follow the existing naming convention scheme.

bigopen()
    function name, follows form of open()
uint
    typedef
bigpos
    struct or class, follows form of pos
sparse_hash_map
    STL-like entity; follows STL naming conventions
LONGLONG_MAX
    a constant, as in INT_MAX

Comments

Comments are absolutely vital to keeping our code readable. The following rules describe what you should comment and where. But remember: while comments are very important, the best code is self-documenting. Giving sensible names to types and variables is much better than using obscure names that you must then explain through comments.

When writing your comments, write for your audience: the next contributor who will need to understand your code. Be generous — the next one may be you!

Comment Style

Use either the // or /* */ syntax, as long as you are consistent.

You can use either the // or the /* */ syntax; however, // is *much* more common. Be consistent with how you comment and what style you use where.

File Comments

Start each file with license boilerplate.

File comments describe the contents of a file. If a file declares, implements, or tests exactly one abstraction that is documented by a comment at the point of declaration, file comments are not required. All other files must have file comments.

Legal Notice and Author Line

Every file should contain license boilerplate. Choose the appropriate boilerplate for the license used by the project (for example, Apache 2.0, BSD, LGPL, GPL).

If you make significant changes to a file with an author line, consider deleting the author line. New files should usually not contain copyright notice or author line.

File Contents

If a .h declares multiple abstractions, the file-level comment should broadly describe the contents of the file, and how the abstractions are related. A 1 or 2 sentence file-level comment may be sufficient. The detailed documentation about individual abstractions belongs with those abstractions, not at the file level.

Do not duplicate comments in both the .h and the .cc. Duplicated comments diverge.

Class Comments

Every non-obvious class declaration should have an accompanying comment that describes what it is for and how it should be used.

```
// Iterates over the contents of a GargantuanTable.
// Example:
//    GargantuanTableIterator* iter = table->NewIterator();
//    for (iter->Seek("foo"); !iter->done(); iter->Next()) {
//      process(iter->key(), iter->value());
//    }
//    delete iter;
class GargantuanTableIterator {
  ...
};
```

The class comment should provide the reader with enough information to know how and when to use the class, as well as any additional considerations necessary to correctly use the class. Document the synchronization assumptions the class makes, if any. If an instance of the class can be accessed by multiple threads, take extra care to document the rules and invariants surrounding multithreaded use.

The class comment is often a good place for a small example code snippet demonstrating a simple and focused usage of the class.

When sufficiently separated (e.g. .h and .cc files), comments describing the use of the class should go together with its interface definition; comments about the class operation and implementation should accompany the implementation of the class's methods.

Function Comments

Declaration comments describe use of the function (when it is non-obvious); comments at the definition of a function describe operation.

Function Declarations

Almost every function declaration should have comments immediately preceding it that describe what the function does and how to use it. These comments may be omitted only if the function is simple and obvious (e.g. simple accessors for obvious properties of the class). These comments should open with descriptive verbs in the indicative mood ("Opens the file") rather than verbs in the imperative ("Open the file"). The comment describes the function; it does not tell the function what to do. In general, these comments do not describe how the function performs its task. Instead, that should be left to comments in the function definition.

Types of things to mention in comments at the function declaration:

- What the inputs and outputs are.
- For class member functions: whether the object remembers reference arguments beyond the duration of the method call, and whether it will free them or not.
- If the function allocates memory that the caller must free.
- Whether any of the arguments can be a null pointer.
- If there are any performance implications of how a function is used.
- If the function is re-entrant. What are its synchronization assumptions?

Here is an example:

```
// Returns an iterator for this table.  It is the client's
// responsibility to delete the iterator when it is done with it,
// and it must not use the iterator once the GargantuanTable object
// on which the iterator was created has been deleted.
//
// The iterator is initially positioned at the beginning of the table.
```

```
//
// This method is equivalent to:
//    Iterator* iter = table->NewIterator();
//    iter->Seek("");
//    return iter;
// If you are going to immediately seek to another place in the
// returned iterator, it will be faster to use NewIterator()
// and avoid the extra seek.
Iterator* GetIterator() const;
```

However, do not be unnecessarily verbose or state the completely obvious.

When documenting function overrides, focus on the specifics of the override itself, rather than repeating the comment from the overridden function. In many of these cases, the override needs no additional documentation and thus no comment is required.

When commenting constructors and destructors, remember that the person reading your code knows what constructors and destructors are for, so comments that just say something like "destroys this object" are not useful. Document what constructors do with their arguments (for example, if they take ownership of pointers), and what cleanup the destructor does. If this is trivial, just skip the comment. It is quite common for destructors not to have a header comment.

Function Definitions

If there is anything tricky about how a function does its job, the function definition should have an explanatory comment. For example, in the definition comment you might describe any coding tricks you use, give an overview of the steps you go through, or explain why you chose to implement the function in the way you did rather than using a viable alternative. For instance, you might mention why it must acquire a lock for the first half of the function but why it is not needed for the second half.

Note you should *not* just repeat the comments given with the function declaration, in the .h file or wherever. It's okay to recapitulate briefly what the function does, but the focus of the comments should be on how it does it.

Variable Comments

In general the actual name of the variable should be descriptive enough to give a good idea of what the variable is used for. In certain cases, more comments are required.

Class Data Members

The purpose of each class data member (also called an instance variable or member variable) must be clear. If there are any invariants (special values, relationships between members, lifetime requirements) not clearly expressed by the type and name, they must be commented. However, if the type and name suffice (int num_events_;), no comment is needed.

In particular, add comments to describe the existence and meaning of sentinel values, such as nullptr or -1, when they are not obvious. For example:

```
private:
// Used to bounds-check table accesses. -1 means
// that we don't yet know how many entries the table has.
int num_total_entries_;
```

Global Variables

All global variables should have a comment describing what they are, what they are used for, and (if unclear) why it needs to be global. For example:

```
// The total number of tests cases that we run through in this
// regression test.
const int kNumTestCases = 6;
```

Implementation Comments

In your implementation you should have comments in tricky, non-obvious, interesting, or important parts of your code.

Explanatory Comments

Tricky or complicated code blocks should have comments before them. Example:

```
// Divide result by two, taking into account that x
// contains the carry from the add.
for (int i = 0; i < result->size(); ++i) {
  x = (x << 8) + (*result)[i];
  (*result)[i] = x >> 1;
  x &= 1;
}
```

Line-end Comments

Also, lines that are non-obvious should get a comment at the end of the line. These end-of-line comments should be separated from the code by 2 spaces. Example:

```
// If we have enough memory, mmap the data portion too.
mmap_budget = max<int64>(0, mmap_budget - index_->length());
if (mmap_budget >= data_size_ &&
    !MmapData(mmap_chunk_bytes, mlock))
  return;  // Error already logged.
```

Note that there are both comments that describe what the code is doing, and comments that mention that an error has already been logged when the function returns.

Function Argument Comments

When the meaning of a function argument is nonobvious, consider one of the following remedies:

- If the argument is a literal constant, and the same constant is used in multiple function calls in a way that tacitly assumes they're the same, you should use a named constant to make that constraint explicit, and to guarantee that it holds.
- Consider changing the function signature to replace a bool argument with an enum argument. This will make the argument values self-describing.
- For functions that have several configuration options, consider defining a single class or struct to hold all the options , and pass an instance of that. This approach has several advantages. Options are referenced by name at the call site, which clarifies their meaning. It also reduces function argument count, which makes function calls easier to read and write. As an added benefit, you don't have to change call sites when you add another option.
- Replace large or complex nested expressions with named variables.
- As a last resort, use comments to clarify argument meanings at the call site.

Consider the following example:

```
// What are these arguments?
const DecimalNumber product = CalculateProduct(values, 7, false, nullptr);
```

versus:

```
ProductOptions options;
options.set_precision_decimals(7);
options.set_use_cache(ProductOptions::kDontUseCache);
const DecimalNumber product =
    CalculateProduct(values, options,
/*completion_callback=*/nullptr);
```

Don'ts

Do not state the obvious. In particular, don't literally describe what code does, unless the behavior is nonobvious to a reader who understands C++ well. Instead, provide higher level comments that describe *why* the code does what it does, or make the code self describing.

Compare this:

```
// Find the element in the vector.  <-- Bad: obvious!
auto iter = std::find(v.begin(), v.end(), element);
if (iter != v.end()) {
  Process(element);
}
```

To this:

```
// Process "element" unless it was already processed.
auto iter = std::find(v.begin(), v.end(), element);
if (iter != v.end()) {
  Process(element);
}
```

Self-describing code doesn't need a comment. The comment from the example above would be obvious:

```
if (!IsAlreadyProcessed(element)) {
  Process(element);
```

```
}
```

Punctuation, Spelling, and Grammar

Pay attention to punctuation, spelling, and grammar; it is easier to read well-written comments than badly written ones.

Comments should be as readable as narrative text, with proper capitalization and punctuation. In many cases, complete sentences are more readable than sentence fragments. Shorter comments, such as comments at the end of a line of code, can sometimes be less formal, but you should be consistent with your style.

Although it can be frustrating to have a code reviewer point out that you are using a comma when you should be using a semicolon, it is very important that source code maintain a high level of clarity and readability. Proper punctuation, spelling, and grammar help with that goal.

TODO Comments

Use TODO comments for code that is temporary, a short-term solution, or good-enough but not perfect.

TODO s should include the string TODO in all caps, followed by the name, e-mail address, bug ID, or other identifier of the person or issue with the best context about the problem referenced by the TODO . The main purpose is to have a consistent TODO that can be searched to find out how to get more details upon request. A TODO is not a commitment that the person referenced will fix the problem. Thus when you create a TODO with a name, it is almost always your name that is given.

```
// TODO(kl@gmail.com): Use a "*" here for concatenation operator.
// TODO(Zeke) change this to use relations.
// TODO(bug 12345): remove the "Last visitors" feature
```

If your TODO is of the form "At a future date do something" make sure that you either include a very specific date ("Fix by November 2005") or a very specific event ("Remove this code when all clients can handle XML responses.").

Formatting

Coding style and formatting are pretty arbitrary, but a project is much easier to follow if everyone uses the same style. Individuals may not agree with every aspect of the formatting rules, and some of the rules may take some getting used to, but it is important that all project contributors follow the style rules so that they can all read and understand everyone's code easily.

To help you format code correctly, we've created a settings file for emacs.

Line Length

Each line of text in your code should be at most 80 characters long.

We recognize that this rule is controversial, but so much existing code already adheres to it, and we feel that consistency is important.

Those who favor this rule argue that it is rude to force them to resize their windows and there is no need for anything longer. Some folks are used to having several code windows side-by-side, and thus don't have room to widen their windows in any case. People set up their work environment assuming a particular maximum window width, and 80 columns has been the traditional standard. Why change it?

Proponents of change argue that a wider line can make code more readable. The 80-column limit is an hidebound throwback to 1960s mainframes; modern equipment has wide screens that can easily show longer lines.

80 characters is the maximum.

A line may exceed 80 characters if it is

- a comment line which is not feasible to split without harming readability, ease of cut and paste or auto-linking -- e.g. if a line contains an example command or a literal URL longer than 80 characters.
- a raw-string literal with content that exceeds 80 characters. Except for test code, such literals should appear near the top of a file.
- an include statement.
- a <u>header guard</u>
- a using-declaration

Non-ASCII Characters

Non-ASCII characters should be rare, and must use UTF-8 formatting.

You shouldn't hard-code user-facing text in source, even English, so use of non-ASCII characters should be rare. However, in certain cases it is appropriate to include such words in your code. For example, if your code parses data files from foreign sources, it may be appropriate to hard-code the non-ASCII string(s) used in those data files as delimiters. More commonly, unittest code (which does not need to be localized) might contain non-ASCII strings. In such cases, you should use UTF-8, since that is an encoding understood by most tools able to handle more than just ASCII.

Hex encoding is also OK, and encouraged where it enhances readability — for example, `"\xEF\xBB\xBF"`, or, even more simply, `u8"\uFEFF"`, is the Unicode zero-width no-break space character, which would be invisible if included in the source as straight UTF-8.

Use the `u8` prefix to guarantee that a string literal containing `\uXXXX` escape sequences is encoded as UTF-8. Do not use it for strings containing non-ASCII characters encoded as UTF-8, because that will produce incorrect output if the compiler does not interpret the source file as UTF-8.

You shouldn't use the C++11 char16_t and char32_t character types, since they're for non-UTF-8 text. For similar reasons you also shouldn't use wchar_t (unless you're writing code that interacts with the Windows API, which uses wchar_t extensively).

Spaces vs. Tabs

Use only spaces, and indent 2 spaces at a time.

We use spaces for indentation. Do not use tabs in your code. You should set your editor to emit spaces when you hit the tab key.

Function Declarations and Definitions

Return type on the same line as function name, parameters on the same line if they fit. Wrap parameter lists which do not fit on a single line as you would wrap arguments in a function call.

Functions look like this:

```
ReturnType ClassName::FunctionName(Type par_name1, Type par_name2) {
  DoSomething();
  ...
}
```

If you have too much text to fit on one line:

```
ReturnType ClassName::ReallyLongFunctionName(Type par_name1, Type par_name2,
                                             Type par_name3) {
  DoSomething();
  ...
}
```

or if you cannot fit even the first parameter:

```
ReturnType
LongClassName::ReallyReallyReallyLongFunctionName(
    Type par_name1,  // 4 space indent
    Type par_name2,
    Type par_name3) {
  DoSomething();  // 2 space indent
  ...
}
```

Some points to note:

- Choose good parameter names.
- A parameter name may be omitted only if the parameter is not used in the function's definition.
- If you cannot fit the return type and the function name on a single line, break between them.
- If you break after the return type of a function declaration or definition, do not indent.
- The open parenthesis is always on the same line as the function name.
- There is never a space between the function name and the open parenthesis.
- There is never a space between the parentheses and the parameters.
- The open curly brace is always on the end of the last line of the function declaration, not the start of the next line.
- The close curly brace is either on the last line by itself or on the same line as the open curly brace.
- There should be a space between the close parenthesis and the open curly brace.
- All parameters should be aligned if possible.

- Default indentation is 2 spaces.
- Wrapped parameters have a 4 space indent.

Unused parameters that are obvious from context may be omitted:

```
class Foo {
public:
  Foo(const Foo&) = delete;
  Foo& operator=(const Foo&) = delete;
};
```

Unused parameters that might not be obvious should comment out the variable name in the function definition:

```
class Shape {
public:
  virtual void Rotate(double radians) = 0;
};

class Circle : public Shape {
public:
  void Rotate(double radians) override;
};

void Circle::Rotate(double /*radians*/) {}
```

```
// Bad - if someone wants to implement later, it's not clear what the
// variable means.
void Circle::Rotate(double) {}
```

Attributes, and macros that expand to attributes, appear at the very beginning of the function declaration or definition, before the return type:

```
ABSL_MUST_USE_RESULT bool IsOk();
```

Lambda Expressions

Format parameters and bodies as for any other function, and capture lists like other comma-separated lists.

For by-reference captures, do not leave a space between the ampersand (&) and the variable name.

```
int x = 0;
auto x_plus_n = [&x](int n) -> int { return x + n; }
```

Short lambdas may be written inline as function arguments.

```
std::set<int> blacklist = {7, 8, 9};
std::vector<int> digits = {3, 9, 1, 8, 4, 7, 1};
digits.erase(std::remove_if(digits.begin(), digits.end(), [&blacklist]
(int i) {
          return blacklist.find(i) != blacklist.end();
       }),
       digits.end());
```

Floating-point Literals

Floating-point literals should always have a radix point, with digits on both sides, even if they use exponential notation. Readability is improved if all floating-point literals take this familiar form, as this helps ensure that they are not mistaken for integer literals, and that the E / e of the exponential notation is not mistaken for a hexadecimal digit. It is fine to initialize a floating-point variable with an integer literal (assuming the variable type can exactly represent that integer), but note that a number in exponential notation is never an integer literal.

```
float f = 1.f;
```

```
long double ld = -.5L;
double d = 1248e6;
```

```
float f = 1.0f;
float f2 = 1;   // Also OK
long double ld = -0.5L;
double d = 1248.0e6;
```

Function Calls

Either write the call all on a single line, wrap the arguments at the parenthesis, or start the arguments on a new line indented by four spaces and continue at that 4 space indent. In the absence of other considerations, use the minimum number of lines, including placing multiple arguments on each line where appropriate.

Function calls have the following format:

```
bool result = DoSomething(argument1, argument2, argument3);
```

If the arguments do not all fit on one line, they should be broken up onto multiple lines, with each subsequent line aligned with the first argument. Do not add spaces after the open paren or before the close paren:

```
bool result = DoSomething(averyveryveryverylongargument1,
                          argument2, argument3);
```

Arguments may optionally all be placed on subsequent lines with a four space indent:

```
if (...) {
  ...
  ...
  if (...) {
    bool result = DoSomething(
        argument1, argument2,  // 4 space indent
```

```
    argument3, argument4);
  ...
}
```

Put multiple arguments on a single line to reduce the number of lines necessary for calling a function unless there is a specific readability problem. Some find that formatting with strictly one argument on each line is more readable and simplifies editing of the arguments. However, we prioritize for the reader over the ease of editing arguments, and most readability problems are better addressed with the following techniques.

If having multiple arguments in a single line decreases readability due to the complexity or confusing nature of the expressions that make up some arguments, try creating variables that capture those arguments in a descriptive name:

```
int my_heuristic = scores[x] * y + bases[x];
bool result = DoSomething(my_heuristic, x, y, z);
```

Or put the confusing argument on its own line with an explanatory comment:

```
bool result = DoSomething(scores[x] * y + bases[x],  // Score heuristic.
              x, y, z);
```

If there is still a case where one argument is significantly more readable on its own line, then put it on its own line. The decision should be specific to the argument which is made more readable rather than a general policy.

Sometimes arguments form a structure that is important for readability. In those cases, feel free to format the arguments according to that structure:

```
// Transform the widget by a 3x3 matrix.
```

```
my_widget.Transform(x1, x2, x3,
            y1, y2, y3,
            z1, z2, z3);
```

Braced Initializer List Format

Format a braced initializer list exactly like you would format a function call in its place.

If the braced list follows a name (e.g. a type or variable name), format as if the {} were the parentheses of a function call with that name. If there is no name, assume a zero-length name.

```
// Examples of braced init list on a single line.
return {foo, bar};
functioncall({foo, bar});
std::pair<int, int> p{foo, bar};

// When you have to wrap.
SomeFunction(
    {"assume a zero-length name before {"},
    some_other_function_parameter);
SomeType variable{
    some, other, values,
    {"assume a zero-length name before {"},
    SomeOtherType{
        "Very long string requiring the surrounding breaks.",
        some, other values},
    SomeOtherType{"Slightly shorter string",
            some, other, values}};
SomeType variable{
    "This is too long to fit all in one line"};
MyType m = {  // Here, you could also break before {.
    superlongvariablename1,
    superlongvariablename2,
```

```
    {short, interior, list},
    {interiorwrappinglist,
        interiorwrappinglist2}};
```

Conditionals

Prefer no spaces inside parentheses. The if and else keywords belong on separate lines.

There are two acceptable formats for a basic conditional statement. One includes spaces between the parentheses and the condition, and one does not.

The most common form is without spaces. Either is fine, but *be consistent*. If you are modifying a file, use the format that is already present. If you are writing new code, use the format that the other files in that directory or project use. If in doubt and you have no personal preference, do not add the spaces.

```
if (condition) {  // no spaces inside parentheses
    ...  // 2 space indent.
} else if (...) {  // The else goes on the same line as the closing brace.
    ...
} else {
    ...
}
```

If you prefer you may add spaces inside the parentheses:

```
if ( condition ) {  // spaces inside parentheses - rare
    ...  // 2 space indent.
} else {  // The else goes on the same line as the closing brace.
    ...
}
```

Note that in all cases you must have a space between the if and the open parenthesis. You must also have a space between the close parenthesis and the curly brace, if you're using one.

```
if(condition) {   // Bad - space missing after IF.
if (condition){   // Bad - space missing before {.
if(condition){    // Doubly bad.

if (condition) {  // Good - proper space after IF and before {.
```

Short conditional statements may be written on one line if this enhances readability. You may use this only when the line is brief and the statement does not use the else clause.

```
if (x == kFoo) return new Foo();
if (x == kBar) return new Bar();
```

This is not allowed when the if statement has an else :

```
// Not allowed - IF statement on one line when there is an ELSE clause
if (x) DoThis();
else DoThat();
```

In general, curly braces are not required for single-line statements, but they are allowed if you like them; conditional or loop statements with complex conditions or statements may be more readable with curly braces. Some projects require that an if must always have an accompanying brace.

```
if (condition)
  DoSomething();  // 2 space indent.

if (condition) {
  DoSomething();  // 2 space indent.
}
```

However, if one part of an if - else statement uses curly braces, the other part must too:

```
// Not allowed - curly on IF but not ELSE
if (condition) {
  foo;
} else
  bar;

// Not allowed - curly on ELSE but not IF
if (condition)
  foo;
else {
  bar;
}

// Curly braces around both IF and ELSE required because
// one of the clauses used braces.
if (condition) {
  foo;
} else {
  bar;
}
```

Loops and Switch Statements

Switch statements may use braces for blocks. Annotate non-trivial fall-through between cases. Braces are optional for single-statement loops. Empty loop bodies should use either empty braces or continue.

case blocks in switch statements can have curly braces or not, depending on your preference. If you do include curly braces they should be placed as shown below.

If not conditional on an enumerated value, switch statements should always have a default case (in the case of an enumerated value, the compiler will warn you if any values are not handled). If the default case should never execute, treat this as an error. For example:

```
switch (var) {
  case 0: {  // 2 space indent
    ...      // 4 space indent
    break;
  }
  case 1: {
    ...
    break;
  }
  default: {
    assert(false);
  }
}
```

Fall-through from one case label to another must be annotated using the ABSL_FALLTHROUGH_INTENDED; macro (defined in absl/base/macros.h). ABSL_FALLTHROUGH_INTENDED; should be placed at a point of execution where a fall-through to the next case label occurs. A common exception is consecutive case labels without intervening code, in which case no annotation is needed.

```
switch (x) {
  case 41:  // No annotation needed here.
  case 43:
    if (dont_be_picky) {
      // Use this instead of or along with annotations in comments.
      ABSL_FALLTHROUGH_INTENDED;
    } else {
      CloseButNoCigar();
```

```
      break;
    }
  case 42:
    DoSomethingSpecial();
    ABSL_FALLTHROUGH_INTENDED;
  default:
    DoSomethingGeneric();
    break;
}
```

Braces are optional for single-statement loops.

```
for (int i = 0; i < kSomeNumber; ++i)
  printf("I love you\n");

for (int i = 0; i < kSomeNumber; ++i) {
  printf("I take it back\n");
}
```

Empty loop bodies should use either an empty pair of braces or `continue` with no braces, rather than a single semicolon.

```
while (condition) {
  // Repeat test until it returns false.
}
for (int i = 0; i < kSomeNumber; ++i) {}  // Good - one newline is also OK.
while (condition) continue;  // Good - continue indicates no logic.
```

```
while (condition);  // Bad - looks like part of do/while loop.
```

Pointer and Reference Expressions

No spaces around period or arrow. Pointer operators do not have trailing spaces.

The following are examples of correctly-formatted pointer and reference expressions:

```
x = *p;
p = &x;
x = r.y;
x = r->y;
```

Note that:

- There are no spaces around the period or arrow when accessing a member.
- Pointer operators have no space after the * or &.

When declaring a pointer variable or argument, you may place the asterisk adjacent to either the type or to the variable name:

```
// These are fine, space preceding.
char *c;
const std::string &str;

// These are fine, space following.
char* c;
const std::string& str;
```

You should do this consistently within a single file, so, when modifying an existing file, use the style in that file.

It is allowed (if unusual) to declare multiple variables in the same declaration, but it is disallowed if any of those have pointer or reference decorations. Such declarations are easily misread.

```
// Fine if helpful for readability.
int x, y;
```

```
int x, *y;  // Disallowed - no & or * in multiple declaration
char * c;  // Bad - spaces on both sides of *
```

```
  const std::string & str;  // Bad - spaces on both sides of &
```

Boolean Expressions

When you have a boolean expression that is longer than the <u>standard line length</u>, be consistent in how you break up the lines.

In this example, the logical AND operator is always at the end of the lines:

```
if (this_one_thing > this_other_thing &&
    a_third_thing == a_fourth_thing &&
    yet_another && last_one) {
  ...
}
```

Note that when the code wraps in this example, both of the && logical AND operators are at the end of the line. This is more common in code, though wrapping all operators at the beginning of the line is also allowed. Feel free to insert extra parentheses judiciously because they can be very helpful in increasing readability when used appropriately. Also note that you should always use the punctuation operators, such as && and ~, rather than the word operators, such as and and compl.

Return Values

Do not needlessly surround the return expression with parentheses.

Use parentheses in return expr; only where you would use them in x = expr; .

```
return result;              // No parentheses in the simple case.
// Parentheses OK to make a complex expression more readable.
return (some_long_condition &&
        another_condition);
```

```
return (value);          // You wouldn't write var = (value);
return(result);          // return is not a function!
```

Variable and Array Initialization

Your choice of = , () , or {} .

You may choose between = , () , and {} ; the following are all correct:

```
int x = 3;
int x(3);
int x{3};
std::string name = "Some Name";
std::string name("Some Name");
std::string name{"Some Name"};
```

Be careful when using a braced initialization list {...} on a type with an std::initializer_list constructor. A nonempty *braced-init-list* prefers the std::initializer_list constructor whenever possible. Note that empty braces {} are special, and will call a default constructor if available. To force the non-std::initializer_list constructor, use parentheses instead of braces.

```
std::vector<int> v(100, 1);  // A vector containing 100 items: All 1s.
std::vector<int> v{100, 1};  // A vector containing 2 items: 100 and 1.
```

Also, the brace form prevents narrowing of integral types. This can prevent some types of programming errors.

```
int pi(3.14);  // OK -- pi == 3.
int pi{3.14};  // Compile error: narrowing conversion.
```

Preprocessor Directives

The hash mark that starts a preprocessor directive should always be at the beginning of the line.

Even when preprocessor directives are within the body of indented code, the directives should start at the beginning of the line.

```
// Good - directives at beginning of line
  if (lopsided_score) {
#if DISASTER_PENDING      // Correct -- Starts at beginning of line
    DropEverything();
# if NOTIFY               // OK but not required -- Spaces after #
    NotifyClient();
# endif
#endif
    BackToNormal();
  }
```

```
// Bad - indented directives
  if (lopsided_score) {
    #if DISASTER_PENDING  // Wrong!  The "#if" should be at beginning of line
    DropEverything();
    #endif                // Wrong!  Do not indent "#endif"
    BackToNormal();
  }
```

Class Format

Sections in public, protected and private order, each indented one space.

The basic format for a class definition (lacking the comments, see Class Comments for a discussion of what comments are needed) is:

```cpp
class MyClass : public OtherClass {
 public:      // Note the 1 space indent!
  MyClass();  // Regular 2 space indent.
  explicit MyClass(int var);
  ~MyClass() {}

  void SomeFunction();
  void SomeFunctionThatDoesNothing() {
  }

  void set_some_var(int var) { some_var_ = var; }
  int some_var() const { return some_var_; }

 private:
  bool SomeInternalFunction();

  int some_var_;
  int some_other_var_;
};
```

Things to note:

- Any base class name should be on the same line as the subclass name, subject to the 80-column limit.
- The public: , protected: , and private: keywords should be indented one space.
- Except for the first instance, these keywords should be preceded by a blank line. This rule is optional in small classes.
- Do not leave a blank line after these keywords.
- The public section should be first, followed by the protected and finally the private section.

- See Declaration Order for rules on ordering declarations within each of these sections.

Constructor Initializer Lists

Constructor initializer lists can be all on one line or with subsequent lines indented four spaces.

The acceptable formats for initializer lists are:

```
// When everything fits on one line:
MyClass::MyClass(int var) : some_var_(var) {
  DoSomething();
}


// If the signature and initializer list are not all on one line,
// you must wrap before the colon and indent 4 spaces:
MyClass::MyClass(int var)
    : some_var_(var), some_other_var_(var + 1) {
  DoSomething();
}


// When the list spans multiple lines, put each member on its own line
// and align them:
MyClass::MyClass(int var)
    : some_var_(var),            // 4 space indent
      some_other_var_(var + 1) { // lined up
  DoSomething();
}

// As with any other code block, the close curly can be on the same
// line as the open curly, if it fits.
MyClass::MyClass(int var)
```

```
    : some_var_(var) {}
```

Namespace Formatting

The contents of namespaces are not indented.

Namespaces do not add an extra level of indentation. For example, use:

```
namespace {

void foo() {  // Correct.  No extra indentation within namespace.
  ...
}

}  // namespace
```

Do not indent within a namespace:

```
namespace {

  // Wrong!  Indented when it should not be.
  void foo() {
    ...
  }

}  // namespace
```

When declaring nested namespaces, put each namespace on its own line.

```
namespace foo {
namespace bar {
```

Horizontal Whitespace

Use of horizontal whitespace depends on location. Never put trailing whitespace at the end of a line.

General

```
void f(bool b) {  // Open braces should always have a space before them.
...
int i = 0;  // Semicolons usually have no space before them.
// Spaces inside braces for braced-init-list are optional.  If you use them,
// put them on both sides!
int x[] = { 0 };
int x[] = {0};

// Spaces around the colon in inheritance and initializer lists.
class Foo : public Bar {
 public:
  // For inline function implementations, put spaces between the braces
  // and the implementation itself.
  Foo(int b) : Bar(), baz_(b) {}  // No spaces inside empty braces.
  void Reset() { baz_ = 0; }  // Spaces separating braces from implementation.
  ...
```

Adding trailing whitespace can cause extra work for others editing the same file, when they merge, as can removing existing trailing whitespace. So: Don't introduce trailing whitespace. Remove it if you're already changing that line, or do it in a separate clean-up operation (preferably when no-one else is working on the file).

Loops and Conditionals

```
if (b) {          // Space after the keyword in conditions and loops.
} else {          // Spaces around else.
}
while (test) {}  // There is usually no space inside parentheses.
switch (i) {
for (int i = 0; i < 5; ++i) {
// Loops and conditions may have spaces inside parentheses, but this
// is rare.  Be consistent.
switch ( i ) {
if ( test ) {
for ( int i = 0; i < 5; ++i ) {
// For loops always have a space after the semicolon.  They may have a space
// before the semicolon, but this is rare.
for ( ; i < 5 ; ++i) {
  ...

// Range-based for loops always have a space before and after the colon.
for (auto x : counts) {
  ...
}
switch (i) {
  case 1:        // No space before colon in a switch case.
    ...
  case 2: break;  // Use a space after a colon if there's code after it.
```

Operators

```
// Assignment operators always have spaces around them.
x = 0;
```

```
// Other binary operators usually have spaces around them, but it's
// OK to remove spaces around factors.  Parentheses should have no
// internal padding.
v = w * x + y / z;
v = w*x + y/z;
v = w * (x + z);

// No spaces separating unary operators and their arguments.
x = -5;
++x;
if (x && !y)
   ...
```

Templates and Casts

```
// No spaces inside the angle brackets (< and >), before
// <, or between >( in a cast
std::vector<std::string> x;
y = static_cast<char*>(x);

// Spaces between type and pointer are OK, but be consistent.
std::vector<char *> x;
```

Vertical Whitespace

Minimize use of vertical whitespace.

This is more a principle than a rule: don't use blank lines when you don't have to. In particular, don't put more than one or two blank lines between functions, resist starting functions with a blank line, don't end functions with a blank line, and be sparing with your use of blank lines. A blank line within a block of code serves like a paragraph break in prose: visually separating two thoughts.

The basic principle is: The more code that fits on one screen, the easier it is to follow and understand the control flow of the program. Use whitespace purposefully to provide separation in that flow.

Some rules of thumb to help when blank lines may be useful:

- Blank lines at the beginning or end of a function do not help readability.
- Blank lines inside a chain of if-else blocks may well help readability.
- A blank line before a comment line usually helps readability — the introduction of a new comment suggests the start of a new thought, and the blank line makes it clear that the comment goes with the following thing instead of the preceding.

Exceptions to the Rules

The coding conventions described above are mandatory. However, like all good rules, these sometimes have exceptions, which we discuss here.

Existing Non-conformant Code

You may diverge from the rules when dealing with code that does not conform to this style guide.

If you find yourself modifying code that was written to specifications other than those presented by this guide, you may have to diverge from these rules in order to stay consistent with the local conventions in that code. If you are in doubt about how to do this, ask the original author or the person currently responsible for the code. Remember that *consistency* includes local consistency, too.

Windows Code

Windows programmers have developed their own set of coding conventions, mainly derived from the conventions in Windows headers and other Microsoft code. We want to make it easy for anyone to understand your code, so we have a single set of guidelines for everyone writing C++ on any platform.

It is worth reiterating a few of the guidelines that you might forget if you are used to the prevalent Windows style:

- Do not use Hungarian notation (for example, naming an integer iNum). Use the naming conventions, including the .cc extension for source files.
- Windows defines many of its own synonyms for primitive types, such as DWORD , HANDLE , etc. It is perfectly acceptable, and encouraged, that you use these types when calling Windows API functions. Even so, keep as close as you can to the underlying C++ types. For example, use const TCHAR * instead of LPCTSTR .
- When compiling with Microsoft Visual C++, set the compiler to warning level 3 or higher, and treat all warnings as errors.
- Do not use #pragma once ; instead use the standard include guards. The path in the include guards should be relative to the top of your project tree.
- In fact, do not use any nonstandard extensions, like #pragma and __declspec , unless you absolutely must.
  Using __declspec(dllimport) and __declspec(dllexport) is allowed; however, you must use them through macros such as DLLIMPORT and DLLEXPORT , so that someone can easily disable the extensions if they share the code.

However, there are just a few rules that we occasionally need to break on Windows:

- Normally we <u>strongly discourage the use of multiple implementation inheritance</u>; however, it is required when using COM and some ATL/WTL classes. You may use multiple implementation inheritance to implement COM or ATL/WTL classes and interfaces.
- Although you should not use exceptions in your own code, they are used extensively in the ATL and some STLs, including the one that comes with Visual C++. When using the ATL, you should define _ATL_NO_EXCEPTIONS to disable exceptions. You should investigate whether you can also disable exceptions in your STL, but if not, it is OK to turn on exceptions in the compiler. (Note that this is only to get the STL to compile. You should still not write exception handling code yourself.)
- The usual way of working with precompiled headers is to include a header file at the top of each source file, typically with a name like StdAfx.h or precompile.h . To make your code easier to share with other projects, avoid including this file explicitly (except in precompile.cc), and use the /FI compiler option to include the file automatically.
- Resource headers, which are usually named resource.h and contain only macros, do not need to conform to these style guidelines.

Parting Words

Use common sense and *BE CONSISTENT*.

If you are editing code, take a few minutes to look at the code around you and determine its style. If they use spaces around their if clauses, you should, too. If their comments have little boxes of stars around them, make your comments have little boxes of stars around them too.

The point of having style guidelines is to have a common vocabulary of coding so people can concentrate on what you are saying, rather than on how you are saying it. We present global style rules here so people know the vocabulary. But local style is also important. If code you add to a file looks drastically different from the existing code around it, the discontinuity throws readers out of their rhythm when they go to read it. Try to avoid this.

OK, enough writing about writing code; the code itself is much more interesting. Have fun!

www.ingramcontent.com/pod-product-compliance
Lightning Source LLC
Chambersburg PA
CBHW082249220526
45469CB00009B/2931